first home
with style

Better Homes and Gardens® Books
Des Moines, Iowa

Better Homes and Gardens® Books
An imprint of Meredith® Books

FIRST HOME WITH STYLE
Editor: Brian Kramer
Project Editor, Writer, and Stylist: Rebecca Jerdee
Contributing Writers: Sharon Overton, Candace Manroe
Contributing Art Director: Sundie Ruppert, Studio G Design
Copy Chief: Terri Fredrickson
Copy and Production Editor: Victoria Forlini
Editorial Operations Manager: Karen Schirm
Managers, Book Production: Pam Kvitne, Marjorie J. Schenkelberg, Rick von Holdt
Contributing Copy Editor: Nancy Ruhling
Contributing Proofreaders: Becky Danley, Sara Henderson, Heidi Johnson
Contributing Photographers: Kim Cornelison, William Hopkins
Indexer: Beverly A. Nightenhelser
Editorial and Design Assistants: Kaye Chabot, Karen McFadden, Mary Lee Gavin

Meredith® Books
Editor in Chief: Linda Raglan Cunningham
Design Director: Matt Strelecki
Executive Editor, Home Decorating and Design: Denise L. Caringer

Publisher: James D. Blume
Executive Director, Marketing: Jeffrey Myers
Executive Director, New Business Development: Todd M. Davis
Executive Director, Sales: Ken Zagor
Director, Operations: George A. Susral
Director, Production: Douglas M. Johnston
Business Director: Jim Leonard

Vice President and General Manager: Douglas J. Guendel

Better Homes and Gardens® Magazine
Vice President/Editor in Chief: Karol DeWulf Nickell
Senior Deputy Editor, Home Design: Oma Blaise Ford

Meredith Publishing Group
President, Publishing Group: Stephen M. Lacy
Vice President-Publishing Director: Bob Mate

Meredith Corporation
Chairman and Chief Executive Officer: William T. Kerr

In Memoriam: E. T. Meredith III (1933–2003)

6 introduction: where to begin

14

where you
cook

60

where you
work

32

where you
eat

78

where you
relax

6

where to begin

dream your rooms

Empty rooms hold the promise of myriad possibilities. In the time between signing on the dotted line and unlocking your new front door, imagine your rooms as they will be. Read books and magazines that inspire decorating dreams. Visit stores to gather information and collect colors and samples to begin your decorating plans.

Nothing matches the excitement and exhilaration of owning your first home. When you turn the key in the lock for the first time, you open the door to the adventures of decorating—at last, home is a place of your own, free of rules imposed by a landlord. It's a good idea to live tentatively in your house for the first year, putting decorating ideas on hold. Think of this as time to hone your decorating plan and slowly get it on track. Also use the time to make structural, plumbing, or electrical repairs, absorb daily life in the house, and see how your rooms live best. Your initial ideas will evolve into better ones.

first things first

Organize what you have and make sure everything in the house functions well. Then make a decorating plan that gives the house your personal signature.

MOVE IN. Arrange the furniture you have and find places for everything that goes into closets and drawers. This will give you clues about where you need to work more storage into your plans.

TAKE STOCK. How does your new house fit your lifestyle? Inventory rooms and how you use them; re-label them and shuffle furnishings to make them function better. Inventory the furniture. How well do the pieces fit? What new pieces do you want?

PLAN ROOMS ON PAPER. It doesn't cost anything to envision your style and completely furnished home or imagine ways to make better use of the furniture you have. Explore options for each room on graph paper, using your handmade furniture templates. Or buy a furniture arranging kit that comes with graph paper and ready-cut templates. Pencil in windows and doors first. Then add major furniture pieces, allowing for traffic zones: 3 feet for interior doors, 4 feet for entries, and at least 30 inches for walkways. For conversation areas, group sofas and chairs a maximum of 8 feet apart. Leave 14 to 18 inches between a sofa and coffee table and at least 3 feet of pullout space behind dining chairs.

REMOVE & REPLACE UNWANTED ELEMENTS. If you don't like the brass switchplates or the bathroom light fixture previous owners left behind, toss them out. Replace

carpet ride

If you want to replace the carpet that came with the house rather than live with it, compare the following carpet qualities before making your purchase:

• **ACRYLIC** carpeting is warm and soft and resists soil and wear. Color and texture may be glossy, and it is prone to crushing. It is moderately priced.

• **NYLON** fibers take dye well for good color ranges. The dull to glossy finish resists mildew, and static-resistant treatments are available.

• **OLEFIN** carpets are durable but limited in color and pattern. They have excellent water resistance and glossy, wavy fibers.

• **POLYESTER** resembles wool in texture and has wool's ability to take a wide range of colors. Crushing of the fibers is possible.

• **WOOL** fibers have excellent texture and resist soil and wear. Wool takes dye well but is expensive and may fade in strong sunlight.

them with ones that appeal to *your* sensibilities. That's part of the freedom of home ownership—you get to decide what goes inside. Don't like the busy fruit-and-flowers wallcovering border someone lovingly attached around the top of the kitchen wall? Steam it off. It's your turn to cook up the color scheme.

WHAT'S UNDERFOOT? Consider any changes you would like to make in flooring. Are your flooring materials appropriate to the climate? For example, thick carpets, rugs, or mats provide insulation in cold climates while stone, concrete, or ceramic floors reduce heat in hot ones. Also, do your floors add to the function of your spaces? For example, thick carpets and rugs soothe and induce an atmosphere of quiet in bedrooms and serene spaces where you want to relax. In active rooms, such as kitchens, baths, or offices, use smooth, tiled, or hardwood floors that wear well and clean up easily.

WHITE IT OUT. Unless you bought the house because you love the way previous owners decorated it, give your house—and yourself—a clean slate. Erase previous owners' paint colors so you can more clearly visualize your own color ideas. Freshen walls with clean, white paint to get the feeling an artist has when encountering a new canvas. If white-painted woodwork, ceilings, and trims are grubby and worn thin, give them new coats of paint too. Consider removing doors for easier traffic flow throughout the house. Store the doors in a basement or attic in case you need to put them back.

REVISE YOUR STORAGE. For a few weeks after the initial move-in, jot down your thoughts about clutter and storage. Think of it as a whole-house organization project. By looking at the big picture, see where to shift items and function—and storage—for better organization. For example, if your small bedroom closet is packed with the clothes you wear, a solution may be to adapt the space with double-hung rods. As you survey your spaces, incorporate storage into your decorating plan.

learn about your style

Prepare yourself to spot the perfect furniture piece or paint color when you see it.

DO RESEARCH. Expose yourself to as many design influences as possible: museums, art galleries, fine-furniture stores, books, and magazines. You may not be able to afford the very best, but you will be able to recognize well-designed furnishings when you see them.

CREATE A STYLE FILE. Tear pages from magazines that inspire you and "paint" a picture of your emerging home style. Be discriminating when you select the tear sheets—avoid cluttering your decorating portrait with too many disparate ideas. Assemble the photographs on scrapbook pages, in pocketed folders, or in a file. List the furnishings and colors in the rooms—they are clues to your style. Collect paint chips and home center samples that please you. Many home stores offer ceramic tile, kitchen counter formica, or wood samples.

QUIZ YOURSELF. Turn the page to find a quiz that will give you some reflections about your decorating style. You'll find a summary at the end of the quiz.

write a budget

In your style file or decorating planner, make a wish list of furnishings you would like to own. Add approximate costs or prices you are willing to pay for them.

SPENDING STYLE. The way you handled money in the past is likely to be the way you will handle it in the future. Are you thrifty or loose with change? Base your decorating plans (and budget) on the way you handle money—don't overestimate your ability to follow through on an unrealistic plan. Apply a realistic budget to your wish list to establish a purchasing time frame and project how much money you will need to carry out the plan. Do everything one step at a time.

Meanwhile, turn to the room-by-room chapters of this book for information and inspiration.

paint to music

Nothing soothes the decorating soul like great tunes. Here are a few colorful ideas from the soundtrack racks, but you'll be sure to create your own collection:

- *TRUE COLORS,* Phil Collins
- *PAINT THE SKY WITH STARS,* Enya
- *BLUE,* Simply Red
- *GOODBYE YELLOW BRICK ROAD,* Elton John
- *INDIGO,* Jim Donovan
- *REALLY BLUE,* Tom Principato
- *NO BLUE THING,* Ray Lynch
- *GREEN,* REM
- *PURPLE RAIN,* Prince and the Revolution
- *SAPPHIRE DREAMS,* Mars Lasar
- *BLONDE ON BLONDE,* Bob Dylan
- *FOREVER BLUE,* Chris Isaak
- *YELLOW SUBMARINE,* The Beatles

commit to color

Trust your eye and instinct to select colors for the first paints you swish over the clean, white walls of your new home. For example, which blue are you? A tranquil sky blue or a high-gloss electric blue? A deep turquoise or a pale Caribbean aquamarine? Or do you prefer to neutralize blue's icy-cold tendencies by pairing it with a rosy pink, a fiery orange, or a sagey green?

11

what's your style?

Left brain/right brain. Type A/Type B. Mars/Venus. Man/Woman. What does this have to do with rearranging the furniture and selecting lamps? More than you think.

If you sometimes feel like the decorating equivalent of Jekyll and Hyde—one day you're mad for floral chintz, the next day you have a penchant for black leather—you can sort it all out. Answer these questions and tally your score, then read your results on the opposite page. (No cheating!) Secure in your newfound self-knowledge, you'll be ready to conquer any design dilemma.

1. What is your dream vacation? a) taking a guided tour of western Europe; b) going on a Caribbean cruise, all amenities included; c) exploring eastern Europe with a Let's Go Guide in hand; d) backpacking in Tibet.

2. You just won the lottery. What is the first thing you do with the money? a) pay off credit card debt; b) make a killing in the stock market (you hope); c) buy your dream car; d) purchase a one-way airline ticket to paradise and travel as long as the mood holds.

3. It is Friday night, and you have no plans for the weekend. How do you feel? a) really anxious; b) slightly frustrated; c) a little relieved; d) ecstatic.

4. Same weekend, but now it is decision time. What to do: a) check the paper for the best entertainment options, then line up companions; b) call a friend for ideas; c) go out anyway—you are bound to run into someone; d) pack a bag and hit the trail, beach, lake, etc.

5. Which term best describes you? a) organized; b) competent; c) independent; d) free-spirited.

6. Where could you picture yourself living? a) stately Georgian-style mini-mansion in the posh suburbs; b) an Arts and Crafts bungalow in a nice, older neighborhood; c) a barn adaptively remade into a house somewhere in suburbia; d) an inner-city warehouse you reshaped into your personal home.

7. For an important job interview, how do you decide what to wear? a) visualize the perfect clothes, then go shopping; b) send an outfit you already own out to be cleaned; c) go shopping and buy whatever catches your eye; d) sift through your closet the morning of the interview.

8. You just started the new novel all your friends are talking about, but it doesn't immediately grab your interest. What do you do? a) finish it anyway; b) commit to the next 50 pages, then decide; c) skip to the end; d) pick up the remote.

9. Which social situation appeals to you most? a) formal dinner party where you know the guests; b) intimate gathering of friends just "hanging out"; c) casual party at a work associate's home, where you can meet new people; d) cocktail party given by a friend of a friend of a friend, whom you know to be slightly crazy.

10. Which combination of furniture fabrics feels right to you? a) chintzes and toiles; b) velvets and linens; c) chenilles and denims; d) kilims and animal prints.

11. "When in Rome," do you: a) do as the Romans do, only better; b) do as the Romans, and that is good enough for you; c) follow your own path and judge the Romans; d) follow your own path and enjoy the Romans along the way.

12. You have time for only one TV show this week. Which will it be? a) *West Wing*; b) *CSI*; c) *Survivor*; d) *Jackass*.

13. Which color scheme is most livable for you? a) one main color plus two accents; b) a monochromatic palette with multiple shades of a single hue; c) a complementary scheme (which features opposites on the color wheel, such as yellow and purple); d) no clearly defined "scheme"—just all the colors in your art and whatever furniture and fabrics happen to strike your fancy.

14. Which chair suits you best? a) 18th-century-style Chippendale; b) classic overstuffed club; c) Eames mid-century modern; d) Philippe Starck polypropylene weather-worthy toy or bubble club chairs.

15. Name your favorite funny guy. a) Jay Leno; b) Adam Sandler; c) Will Ferrell; d) Tom Green.

find yourself here

For every question answered with "a", you score 10 points; give yourself 8 points for each "b" answer; 6 points for "c"; 4 points for "d".

a

If you scored 128 to 150 points, you are the classic Type A, left brain, Mars practitioner of home design. You appreciate a home that is planned to the nth degree, with nothing left to guesswork. You find serenity and comfort in the familiar. Traditional design isn't necessarily your thing, but classics are. Your home must be functional and hard-working, as well as beautiful. You won't settle for less. Adequate, well-organized storage is as important as aesthetics to you—no scattered CDs and videos in your humble abode! Your highly competitive nature also means you keep up with the latest products and looks in decorating to ensure your position at the top. You bring confidence to design, but face it—you like it scripted. The less opportunity for spontaneity, the better. You have no problem consulting the latest design and decorating books and magazines provided they are the best.

b

If you scored 105 to 127 points, you are a toned-down Type A. You appreciate the familiar and an organized approach, but you won't fall to pieces if your partner hauls a flea market retro find home to replace one of your contemporary chairs. You are not hung up about appearances, although you like to make a good show. More important to you is comfort. You love putting on your favorite clothes and settling into a comfy chair. Your taste may be contemporary or a little country or traditional—but it is always moderate. If contemporary is your thing, it's not too cutting-edge; if you are more a traditionalist, you are not rigid about it. People enjoy your home for its easygoing order and compelling comfort. Everything feels in place—a source of serenity—yet nothing feels hands-off (another source of serenity).

c

If you scored 83 to 104 points, you are a go-with-the-flow home decorator. You don't get uptight about change, but embrace it. You are experimental without going too far out on a limb. Convention still matters to you, but far less than it does to most. You peruse decorating magazines for inspiration, then follow your heart. You enjoy your own creativity and use resources to tap it. You shy away, however, from anything that shocks. Art that is controversial or color combinations that are potentially jolting are outside your comfort zone. Your home appeals with its spontaneity and its honesty. Fresh and uncontrived, it shows who you really are, not just who you want to appear to be. If you love Elvis art on black velvet, you go with it—and not because it is hip to be kitsch but because it is hip to be you. You allow your instincts to lead you to unexplored places, but you never force it. You are content with yourself, and your home shows it.

d

If you scored 60 to 82 points, you are a right brain, Venus decorator at his or her most freewheeling, no-holds-barred best. You thrive on change, spontaneity, and an absence of rules. Found objects comprise some of your collections and may rest alongside expensive heirlooms. To you, the juxtaposition of opposites means excitement. Interesting form and texture are more compelling to you than recognized brands or pedigrees. You don't mind shock appeal and will go to great lengths to shake things up. Thinking outside the box as you do, it is no surprise that you avoid linear arrangements and formal symmetry; piles and layers of objects massed asymmetrically for free-form dimension are your preference. Even your slipcovers puddle. You don't just toss pillows on the sofa—you toss them on the floor and call it alternative seating. If you are a contemporary fan, your furnishings are out there, at the edge, startlingly. If you are a traditionalist (not likely), it manifests as a magnificent period piece married with something wildly abstract and modern. But you are not so much a this- or that-style decorator as you are a little-of-this, little-of-that—eclectic to the max. You also love color. Even if your furnishings, windows, and walls are monochromatic or neutral (again, not likely), your art and accessories spice up the look with shots of pure pigment. Multiple pattern mixes with a touch of the exotic appeal to you, and ethnic art rates especially high on your list. Nicks and scrapes, to you, symbolize artistic imperfections. Friends gravitate to your place for an energy fix.

where you COOK

Whether your notion of cooking is concocting a 28-step recipe with the expertise of a Cordon Bleu chef or merely popping a frozen pizza in the oven, preparing a meal brings people together. For many, friends and family typically hang out in the kitchen during food prep time, offering help or conversation. And between meal preparation and cleanup, your kitchen table is likely to attract everything from casual gatherings to a drift of bills, junk mail, keys, art projects, the workings of a home business, and plans for home improvement.

Is your new kitchen fitted or unfitted? If you moved into a house with a fitted kitchen, you inherited built-in appliances and cabinetry. You may want to change them, depending on how you use a kitchen. Most popular and least expensive, the fitted kitchen is arranged in one of five ways: the two-sided galley, the one-sided in-line kitchen, the U shape, the L shape, or the island unit surrounded by cabinetry. The unfitted kitchen, with either traditional or contemporary freestanding storage, is the *au courant* style. The advantage to an unfitted arrangement is that you can invest in high-quality appliances and furnishings to take with you when you move.

This chapter provides glimpses of first home kitchens as well as insider information to help you design the kitchen of your dreams.

to fit or not to fit? that is the question

To fulfill your needs for storage, cooking, cleaning, crossing paths, communicating, entertaining, bill paying, planning, and list making, you may prefer a fitted kitchen. However, a blend of fitted and unfitted furnishings is likely to work best. The new kitchen, *opposite,* is a fitted kitchen with Shaker-style cabinets, but for a stylish "unfitted" update, one section is built to look like a freestanding hutch with glass doors, a high wood top, beaded-board backing, and feet.

imagine
the perfect kitchen

function junctions

in-line kitchen with a view

Stripped of upper cupboards, this simple galley kitchen provides an unobstructed view of the outdoors. An extended counter runs all the way to the wall in the eating area to increase storage on the lower level. For easy access to below-counter storage and the distinctive imprint of style like this, remove swinging cabinet doors and hang space-saving linen skirts on curtain rods.

lighting your kitchen

Upper cabinets sometimes prevent light from entering a fitted kitchen. To lift and brighten the space, paint the walls gloss

white enamel and choose white countertops, cabinets, appliances, and accessories. To further illuminate the space, set

a lamp on the counter and plug it in.

what you need

large appliances
range/cooktop/oven, ventilation system, refrigerator/freezer

worktop
counter, cutting board, or table

sink

storage
cabinets or cupboards, rolling cart

lighting
overhead, stove light, sink light, pendant over counter or table

small appliances
microwave, coffeemaker, handheld portable electric mixer, toaster, starter blender

range-top cookware
1-quart covered saucepan, 2-quart covered saucepan, 4- or 6-quart Dutch oven, 10-inch ovenproof skillet with cover

preparation & cooking gadgets
bottle opener, can opener, chef's knife, glass measuring cup, colander, corkscrew, meat thermometer, timer, ladle, long-handle fork, pancake turner, paring knife, cutting board, rubber spatulas, serrated knife, set of dry measuring cups, set of measuring spoons, set of mixing bowls, knife sharpener, slotted spoon, tongs, utility knife, vegetable peeler, wire cooling racks, wooden spoons

bakeware
2-quart rectangular baking dish, 8 x 8- or 9 x 9-inch square baking dish, 15 x 10 x 1-inch baking pan, 8-inch round baking pan, two baking sheets, 8 x 4 x 2-inch loaf pan or dish

what you'll want

large appliance upgrades
refrigerator/freezer; range

dishwasher

storage upgrade
fitted or unfitted cabinets

flooring upgrade
terra-cotta tile, ceramic tile, rubber, vinyl, linoleum, or hardwood

table and chairs

garbage disposal

trash compactor

cutting board island on wheels

recycling center

upgraded lighting

electric can opener

espresso machine

coffee grinder

top-of-the-line mixer

top-of-the-line blender

steamers

waffle iron

pasta maker; pasta server

salt and pepper mill

makeover
on a budget

paneling that isn't

Like white bread, white box houses often lack textures and interesting surfaces. Here's a looks-like paneling idea you can create for the price of moldings—simply apply white-painted wood moldings over sheetrocked walls. For the horizontal ledge, attach undercap molding to the wall 20 inches below the ceiling and top it with doorstop. For the vertical bands, attach screen molding strips, spacing them 24 inches apart.

Some kitchens require reconstruction. Others function perfectly, needing little more than a cosmetic lift. If your fitted kitchen is only 20 or 30 years old and in good shape and working condition, give it a simple makeover with surface treatments to lift that tired look.

skin-deep beauty

Apply one or more of these beauty treatments to give your fitted kitchen a lighter, younger look.

WALL COLOR. With lots of activity going on in your kitchen, it is best to keep walls simple. White paint is ideal for a sense of freshness and hygiene while a cool, airy blue, cornsilk yellow, or peachy pink gives a light, bright atmosphere. For drama in a modern stainless-steel kitchen, choose zesty lime or a hot pink wall color.

CUPBOARD FACELIFTS. Replace doors and drawer fronts to transform the look for much less than the cost of a remodel. Because most built-in kitchens are produced in standard dimensions, you easily can replace old doors with new ones. A less expensive option: fresh paint on doors and cupboard frameworks. White cupboards and cabinets look best with white appliances and make a unified, clean, and modern look—consider it the best choice for a first home. Later, as your decorative style emerges, you can change the white canvas to your signature color or do a remodel.

WORKTOP PEELS. Relieve your worktop of its worn-down surface and replace it with one of these options:

Formica counters are the least expensive and, in general, the most maintenance free. You'll find them in a host of colors and patterns.

Ceramic tile worktops are practical but have one drawback—maintaining the grout between the tiles.

Solid wood worktops, usually made from hardwood, are better than lacquered types, which don't wear well.

Stainless-steel counters require extra care to keep up their modern, restaurant-style looks.

FLOOR STRIP. What lies beneath your floor covering? Peel back the layer(s) to decide whether you need to strip the floor or layer on do-it-yourself tile. Vinyl and linoleum, available in a variety of colors and patterns, come in sheets or tiles that are easy to keep clean. Terra-cotta or ceramic tiles provide durable surfaces with textural interest; choose tile with textured, nonglossy surfaces to avoid slipping. Wood flooring—hardwood, laminate, or synthetic—is a warm and comfortable option.

kitchen jewelry

Add metal accents to highlight a resurfaced kitchen. Metals—gold, brass, silver, stainless steel, galvanized tin, nickel, or chrome—work wonders to highlight cupboard doors and fixtures. Furniture or lighting fixtures may have shiny metal parts too. A good rule: Choose one metal for the scheme and, as much as possible, stick to it when adding hardware.

Turn the page for more details and ideas that can add decorative accents in your kitchen.

style on a budget

Use a patio table and chairs in a starter kitchen for a bistro cafe effect. Affordable yet stylish, they can be moved out to a patio when you upgrade the furniture for your kitchen.

postcards from the edge

Organize a mail and key stop on the end cap of a row of

upper cabinets. If you have space for it, hang a bulletin

board with pushpins, a calendar, or a metallic memo board

with magnets. Another creative idea: Paint the wall around

your wall phone with a glossy enamel; write priority phone

numbers on the wall in pencil. To update, wash the wall

with detergent.

cupboard accents

Remove a few upper cabinet doors to give a narrow kitchen

a wider sense of itself. Then set off the revealed shelves with

a decorative treatment of paint, wallcovering, and your most

attractive kitchen supplies. On plain cupboard doors, which

hide clutter, add insets of the same wallcovering. Finish the

edges of each inset with a mitered frame cut from screen

molding (buy a miter box from a home center).

interior seduction

All that glitters is not gold. It could be the clean and shiny dishes gleaming on your open kitchen shelves. Or it could be the sunlight reflecting off the narrow mirror panels you laid along the back walls of the cupboard. Home center mirror panels invite the eye inside and add light to the deep spaces of a cupboard without doors. They also create reflections, making it appear as if you have more dishware than you do.

wide-open spaces

25

organize
with style

metal-clad drawers

Remember wrapping schoolbooks in
craft paper? Use sheets of galvanized
tin to jazz up drawer fronts. Just fold,
glue the edges securely to the drawer
with construction adhesive, and screw
on new metal pulls.

white works

White is a stage for spotlighting
natural textures and tones. If this guy
would move, you could see how it sets
off a knobby rattan side chair,
especially when the chair is balanced
by the wood frame on top of the
cupboard. A freestanding windowed
cupboard is *haute couture* in a
kitchen, especially when you have
marvelous dishware to show off.

edgy ledges

Use the metal-clad drawer wrapping technique, *opposite,* to delineate and add gloss to open cupboard shelves. First measure and cut shelf liners from sheets of galvanized tin with tin snips. Then fold the metal over the shelves, press the folds with your fingers, and glue the liners securely in place with construction adhesive.

behind clothes doors

Enclose laundry appliances in or near your kitchen with off-the-rack shower curtains hung on cable. This softens the hard edges of a kitchen and avoids swinging doors that get in the way.

hard rack cafe

Roll a cabinet-height food
service cart, loaded with
chips, dips, and champagne
buckets, from kitchen to living
room and back—wheels
make it easy. Use the cart as
kitchen storage when the
party's over. Choose a cafe
rack made of materials that
blend with your kitchen for an
extension to the end of a
worktop counter. Or store a
vintage cart in a pantry.

Trendy, unfitted kitchens with portable freestanding units add up to cool, industrial chic that moves on when you move out. A stainless-steel bar lets you perch instead of sit over your morning mocha java. At countertop height, it doubles as a workstation. Assemble RTA (ready-to-assemble) units for inexpensive storage—translucent plastic sliding doors on the cabinets let you see when the cupboard is bare. The best part: You still can afford groceries.

flex appeal

sugar on a roll

After appearing inside cupboards for decades, here the lazy Susan is again—in clear plastic. To keep your countertop condiments in line but always accessible, shop garden stores for plant dollies made in materials to match your kitchen style. This lightweight, see-through platter on wheels fits modern worktops; metal or wood dollies suit traditional ones.

list your needs

Answer these questions to define how you want your kitchen to work:

• Does your command-central kitchen lack space for paperwork and message exchanging?

• How big a role does cooking play? Do you get derailed in a narrow galley while sharing the cook space? Are you an experimental cook who stores exotic ingredients?

• Do you shop for groceries often and in small amounts or tackle the task in one big trip that requires deep storage for items you buy in bulk?

• Do you eat in your kitchen and lack storage for tableware? Is your kitchen accessible to outdoor dining?

• What else goes on in your kitchen? Do you have children who need space for homework, friends who hang out while you cook, or laundry that keeps piling up?

lay out a plan

Draw your kitchen floor plan on graph paper and put in door and window placements, stove vent, plumbing connections, and electrical sockets. Bring your floor plan to kitchen stores and showrooms as a reference when you're looking for new appliances.

WORK A TRIANGLE. Base your kitchen plan on the age-old principle of the work triangle that is shaped by a convenient track between three points—the stove, refrigerator, and sink. For the best function between each hot, cold, and wet junction, keep the distances short. A track length of no more than 24 feet is ideal. Allow for adequate counter space between the three stops with at least 3 feet between stove and fridge.

STORAGE. What kind of storage do you need? Is your cookbook collection growing? Do you have a penchant for gee-whiz cooking gadgets? Collections tend to grow, so allow for them as you plan.

Choose cupboards and fitted cabinets with adjustable shelves and sliding doors that take up less space. Roll-out basket shelves give you easy access to items deep inside; lazy Susans rotate to let you select what you need. Save money with ready-to-assemble cabinetry you assemble yourself. Hire a professional installer.

accessorize

Personal style is established when you select new appliances, storage pieces, and furniture. Follow through with accessories that sparkle with your personality and signature. Embellish your cooking space with a couple of no-nonsense kitchen-related items that spell out your mix-don't-match style. For example, an oversize modern clock or new restaurant stools combined with vintage, freestanding cupboard units create an unexpected blend of accessories that add up to a lively, warm kitchen space that's all about you.

Minimize the number of items on your worktops. Go for a few large-scale items that offer more impact than a dozen small things. If you have a large number of small essentials you want to keep handy on a wall, arrange them together.

lighting

• **PENDANTS:** From incandescent bulbs with vintage glass shades to ultrafuturistic halogen cones that pack brightness into tiny fixtures, hanging pendants are popular for ceiling fixtures. Place pendants over an island or countertop, where low-hanging fixtures don't interfere with traffic flow.

• **TUBE LIGHTS** (miniature white lights in plastic) are easy to use in coves above cabinetry. Simply plug them in and lay them across the tops of the cabinets.

• **UPLIGHTS** or sconces play up the nonstandard features of architecturally interesting ceilings.

• **DOWNLIGHTS** or recessed fixtures light the kitchen in a general way, supplementing task lights.

• **STRIP LIGHTS** under cabinets and shelves light tasks on the counter or accent a display of dishes in a freestanding cupboard.

• **TRACKS** with movable fixtures provide general light or can be aimed at specific areas for accents.

plan
your kitchen's future

safe on the range

For a household with children, select a stove with controls on the top rather than the

front. Work at the back burners whenever possible and keep fabrics away from the stove.

If you build or remodel, choose slip-resistant flooring. Have electrical outlets connected to

ground fault circuit interrupters. Keep an ABC-rated, 5-pound fire extinguisher handy.

31

32

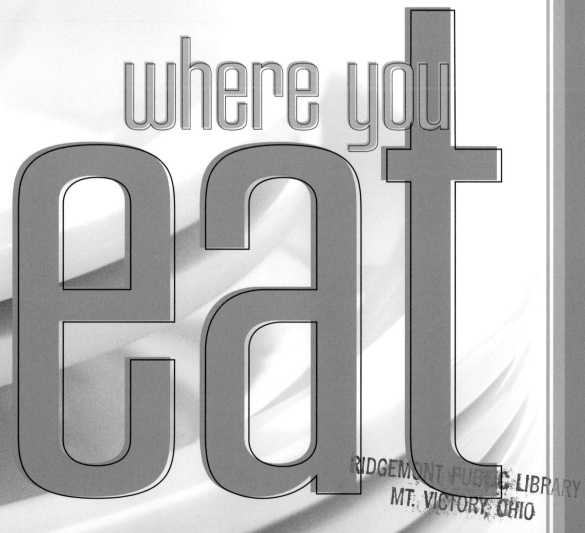

where you
eat

In today's broadband world, a dining room is a welcome stop. It's where you regroup, refuel, and reconnect with family and friends before going out again.

Chances are the first meal in your first home was little more than Chinese takeout and beverages balanced on a cardboard moving carton. However far from your dream of the ideal dining space, the convivial occasion was as photo-album worthy as the "before" pictures you took to mark how you entered the world of homeownership.

For now, the dream of a formal dining room may be on hold. One reason may be that it's not a top priority for you and the way you plan to use your new home. Another may be budget constraints. Sharing food with family and friends, even in the humblest circumstances, is one of the more enjoyable pleasures of life. No matter what your means, set up an eating spot that serves you and those who will grace your table.

Some homes do not have dining rooms; some have dining areas at the end of an open-plan living room. If you have one, you can move right in with what you have and decorate windows and walls. If your first home doesn't have a dining room, you'll have fun inventing eating spaces to meet your needs. Turn the pages of this chapter to learn how.

34

opposites attract

Imagine mixing contemporary metal chairs with a traditional wooden trestle table. The bold pairing of two such opposing styles is an enticing decorating idea that has worked in dining rooms for decades. If the contradictory style appeals to you, but you can't afford expensive furniture right now, practice pairing opposites with small investments in tableware—a few pieces at a time to work with your dining room of the future. Get the look with mismatched white china and contemporary stainless-steel flatware. Or collect funky, old silver flatware and team it with sparkling new white china.

dare to dream

no dining room on the floor plan?

Eat in the living room on a table that doubles as a home office work surface or catchall for keys and books. A round table usually works best and secondhand furniture fits the first home budget. These reupholstered chairs, purchased for $7 each, were once covered in orange vinyl. The nonwood table and once-dark storage unit on the far wall wear new coats of enamel paint.

start
with what you have

eat in the kitchen

Sometimes the most logical place for meeting and eating is in the room where you cook. To keep a small cooking/eating room from looking overcrowded, choose a bar-height table that shows off lots of floor space. Simple furniture design and finishes are best for making a space look larger. Here, white-painted bar-height chairs and a birch assemble-it-yourself Shaker-style table keep dining light and right for two.

yes, dine in bed

OK, so cheese puffs and Chinese takeout can get a little messy. That's where white sheets are the most practical tablecloth—you can bleach them and hang them to dry outside for more whitening and extra crispness. The real benefit is the ease and spontaneity of setting up a special moment at the end of a busy day.

eating in

Eating and sleeping get the top two spots on the list of priorities for living, so you're

likely to make your bedroom the first place of comfort in your new home. If you lack a

sofa or comfortable chairs, your bed also will supply the best seats in the house for

television viewing. Naturally, eating follows. When your bedroom is the first room in the

house you furnish, make it more dining room stylish with a low coffee table

surrounded by floor pillows. It will handle food and drinks you don't want to spill on

your bed linens. Here, Moroccan mint tea served in gold-painted glasses (check

antiques stores) makes a soothing toddy and an exotic end to an ordinary day.

unassigned seating

dine al fresco

Spread out on a three-season porch, patio, balcony, or terrace when you don't have a dining room. It's a natural space for dining, weather permitting. While the expected plastic patio set may be the least expensive choice for outdoor furniture, consider hand-me-down or secondhand wood furniture for a more stylish option. Woods will weather but take on a charming patina when left outdoors. If your area is uncovered, protect wood furniture with exterior deck paint. This terrace dining room is set with rustic pine furniture, a sisal area rug, a side service bar, and a panel of outdoor fabric that blocks the hot afternoon sun and makes the space a little more private.

what you need

starter table
kitchen, patio, side, or coffee table; ottoman, counter or TV trays

starter chairs

simple storage
ledge, shelving, or roll-about cart

overhead lighting

casual place mats

paper napkins

salt and pepper shakers

casual dinner and side plates

soup bowls

basic pitcher, glasses

coffee mugs

basic serving bowls and platters

flatware, serving pieces:
salad servers, 2 or 3 large serving spoons,
slotted serving spoon, serving fork, carving set

insulated picnic backpack

plastic picnic cloth

white tealights

pillar candles

basic flower vases
bud, urn, cylinder

what you'll want

dream table

dream chairs

storage upgrade
hutch, sideboard, armoire, or entertainment unit

white tablecloth

cloth napkins

napkin rings

formal dinnerware

crystal pitchers

elegant stemware, glasses

formal serving bowls and platters

formal flatware, serving pieces

designer salt and pepper shakers

dressy dessert plates

coffee service

name card holders

crystal flower vases

candelabra

classic candleholders

lighting
raise-and-lower pendant, chandelier, or table lamps

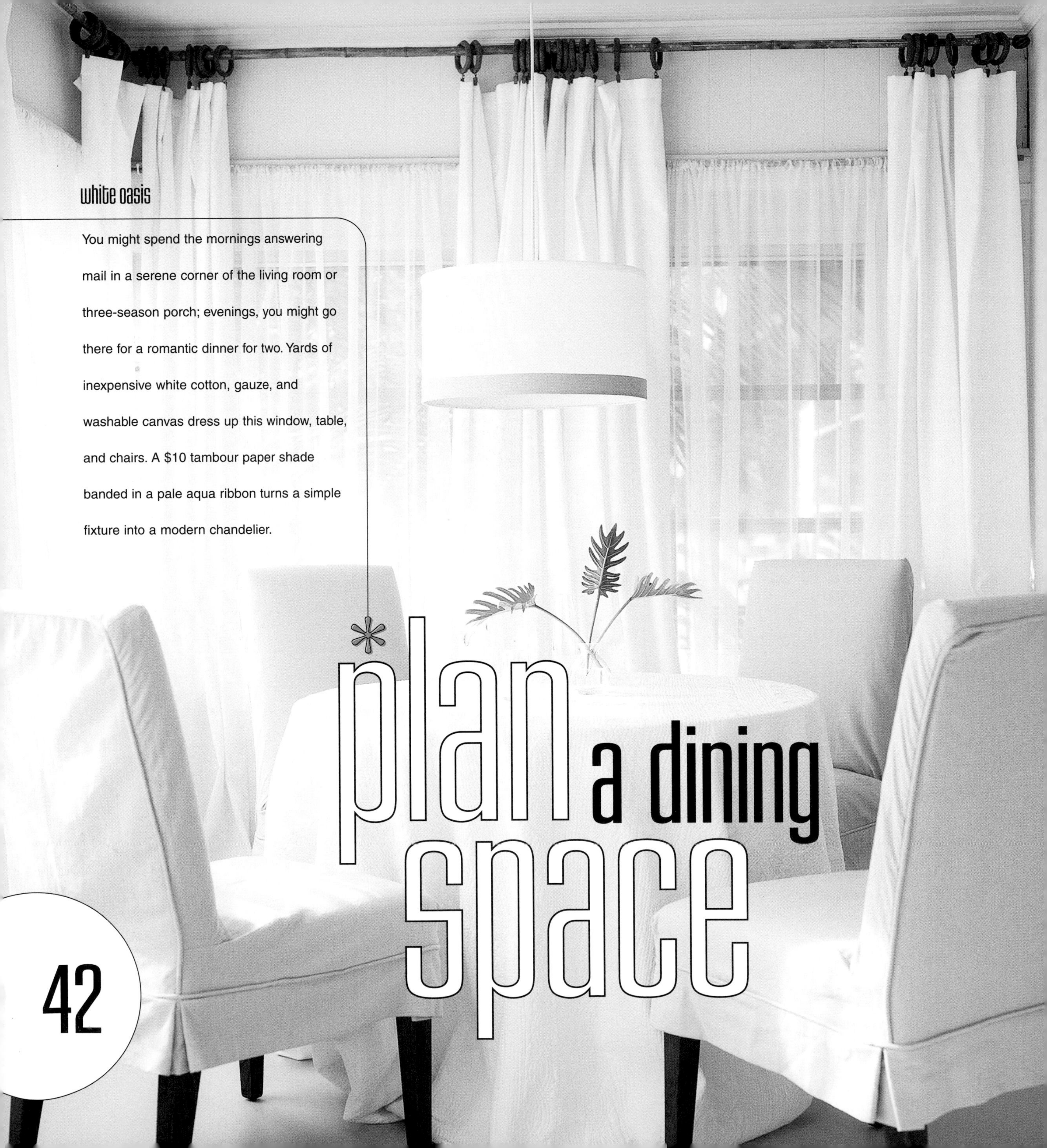

white oasis

You might spend the mornings answering mail in a serene corner of the living room or three-season porch; evenings, you might go there for a romantic dinner for two. Yards of inexpensive white cotton, gauze, and washable canvas dress up this window, table, and chairs. A $10 tambour paper shade banded in a pale aqua ribbon turns a simple fixture into a modern chandelier.

plan a dining space

With a dining room or dining area, you automatically might move in a table and chairs and begin plans for decorating windows, walls, and lighting. Or, if you like to entertain your friends casually, you could decide to turn the "dining space" into a home office or bedroom and dine around the house impromptu-style—like first home owners without formal dining rooms.

finding space

Without a dining room, the challenge is to make another room or table surface work as your dining table. For easy access, a good rule is to leave 3 feet between it and the closest wall. Leave more than 3 feet between the table and a storage piece or in front of doors.

IN THE LIVING ROOM. Arrange living room seating pieces in a way that allows space for dining. Could a small table squeeze into a window area at one end of your room or in the middle of the room in front of the fireplace? Could a large coffee table also serve as your dining table? Consider this: New and stylish TV trays are nothing like your grandmother's. Use them as separate mini-tables; for entertaining, place them in a line together as a buffet on one side of the room and let guests balance plates in their laps. Another idea: Two round side tables can serve as dining tables between a pair of love seats.

IN THE ENTRANCE OR SECOND BEDROOM. Any walk-through room is a candidate for dining if it's adjacent to the kitchen. For example, dine in a walk-through bedroom if you don't need it for sleeping. Or set a round table in a large entrance. On ordinary days, the table catches keys and mail, but you can clear it easily for sit-down dining or a casual buffet, where guests find seats anywhere in the house. Keep folding chairs and washable slipcovers in the closet for dressing up the "dining room" and cover a good carpet with a washable area rug to guard against spills and stains.

IN THE KITCHEN. Cooking and eating go together, so kitchens always do double (and triple) duty. For style in a small galley kitchen, set up an outdoor bistro table with folding chairs. Or hang a half-round table on a kitchen wall for flip-up dining; pull up a stool as needed. Use a rolling cart/cutting board as a dining surface in a kitchen space or bring barstools up to a counter (it's best if the counter has an overhang). Keep a basket of tabletop items for easy transport to the surface.

IN THE OFFICE. If your desk is in the hub of the house, you can clear the work surface occasionally to serve as a walk-by buffet or set it up as a wet bar.

dining light

Accent lighting that focuses softly on the table creates an atmosphere for dining and promotes lingering.

PENDANT. One inexpensive option is a paper lampshade on a light cord. Try a white import-store globe attached to a coordinating corded fixture that hangs from a hook in the ceiling and plugs into a wall socket.

CHANDELIER. Update a chandelier by painting it white, adding new white shades, or fitting it with a dimmer switch to control brightness.

CANDLES. For visual drama and easy but elegant style, nothing matches candlelight. Tealights placed at each setting are an inexpensive alternative to candleholders.

dining tables

Choose the table size that fits your space, family, and entertaining needs. Flip-top tables, tables with leaves, or drop-leaf styles are options when a larger table is needed for special occasions.

ROUND: SIZE/SEATING
- 36-inch diameter seats 2
- 40-inch diameter seats 4
- 56-inch diameter seats 8

SQUARE: SIZE/SEATING
- 38-inch square seats 4

RECTANGULAR/OBLONG: SIZE/SEATING
- 36x60 seats 6
- 36x72 seats 6 to 8
- 36x84 seats 6 to 8
- 48x96 seats 8 to 10
- 48x132 seats 12

When buying a new dining room table and chairs, you'll benefit from the furniture-buying information below. You can also brush up your knowledge of wood.

shopping tips

Tables for a formal dining room, informal dining room, or kitchen need to be large enough to allow elbowroom for comfort without overcrowding. Allow 24 to 30 inches per person and at least 30 inches across the table. Standard dining table height is 29 to 30 inches.

Check leg placement on any table that will be used for seating. A leg at or near each corner, a center pedestal, multiple pedestals, or trestles are stable and common. Complex and artful shapes also work well, as long as the leg placement doesn't interfere with comfortable seating. Lean on the table from all angles to see whether it tips or wobbles.

Dining chairs need fairly upright backs so diners can sit comfortably close to the table and have the support of the chair back. Avoid chairs with legs that splay widely. They fit awkwardly at the table, are easy to trip over, and may be weaker than others. Slide chairs up to the table to see how easily they move in and out. Avoid metal chairs that look beautiful but weigh too much for easy sliding. Check to see whether the chairs fit easily with the table. Are the arms low enough so that the chairs slide under the table? For passage and serving while people are seated at the dining table, allow 24 inches behind each chair.

Sit at the table. Determine whether there is adequate space between the apron (the skirtlike extension around the underside of the table) and your thighs. If you decide to use lower chairs because of the apron depth, check that the chairs are high enough for dining.

buying wood furniture

The quality of wood furniture depends on the material, construction techniques, and finish. Hardwood, softwood, or composite wood is used in furniture construction. Some furniture is constructed from solid wood, but a large percentage of new pieces is manufactured from veneers, which are thin sheets of decorative wood laid over another building material.

Hardwoods are more durable than softwoods and typically more expensive. Colors range widely among woods—even those of the same type—and various woods can be stained or bleached to alter their original color. Composite woods are used for shelving, on the back of furniture pieces, and for some modern styles of furniture.

HARDWOODS. Among the hardwoods, cherry, maple, mahogany, oak, teak, and walnut are prized for quality furniture. However, cherry and maple are considered more difficult to craft than other hardwoods. Hardwood choices generally are a matter of appearance, furniture style, budget, and preference.

Birch. Light tan to almost white, it has a good resistance to shrinking, swelling, and warping; it takes stains well and often is stained to resemble mahogany, walnut, or cherry. Birch is hard to work with for intricate details, so it is commonly used in furniture with simple lines.

Oak. This tough, hard, durable wood carries a distinctive growth pattern produced by prominent medullary rays. Common to furnituremaking, it also is easily recognized by its yellow-brown coloring.

Cherry. Pale yellow to deep red, this wood is much used for fine cabinetry and prized for its resistance to shrinking, swelling, and warping.

Maple. Hard, light-colored, and close-grained, maple is used extensively for flooring, furniture, and small items such as handles and turnings. It is light brown to grayish yellow.

Poplar. Light tan, often with pink- and green-tinted streaks, poplar is one of the weaker hardwoods. It has the same shrinkage rating as teak. It is easy to work with and best for interior furniture parts.

SOFTWOODS. More available than hardwoods, these woods typically are less expensive. They can be a good choice, depending on use and preference.

choose
a table & chairs

the flip side

Instead of buying a single table for an open-plan dining area, purchase two wood flip-top ones. For everyday use, set the two side by side in their closed positions and gather wood-and-wicker chairs around them. Turn the page to see how they'll flip their lids for company.

style on a budget

Shop discount stores and look for high style at bargain-basement prices. For more savings, buy flat-pack furniture and assemble the pieces yourself.

when company comes

guess who's coming to dinner

Turn the tables for a dinner crowd of eight. Here two flip-top tables, shown on page 45, are folded out and repositioned end to end in the dining/living room. The folding chairs come down from hooks on the wall to mix with the wicker chairs. The tabletops are unified with a long white cloth made from inexpensive 45-inch-wide looks-like-linen yardage. Black cloth napkins accentuate the length of the table and give it rhythm and style.

Double the size of a flip-top table with a flick of the wrist. Simply rotate the doubled-up top a half-turn on its base and open it.

been mixed together and pressure-treated. It is a common component of inexpensive furniture that is covered with laminate or veneer. It splits easily, and often the laminate pops loose when the particleboard swells and shrinks with moisture changes.

Medium Density Fiberboard: "MDF" for short, this particleboard improvement is ground much more finely than particleboard and assembled under higher pressure. This denser material machines better; its edges look more like wood. Because of its density, MDF swells and shrinks less than particleboard.

unfinished tables & chairs

Do you like the idea of buying inexpensive unfinished furniture to finish yourself? What do you think of refinishing old pieces? Consider these paint and stain options when you take on a project.

BLEACH lightens the color of wood. Some bleached woods become almost white while still showing grain. Bleached-out woods are a trend that updates pieces of old furniture. Apply clear lacquer over bleached wood to protect it.

ENAMEL PAINT hides the color and grain of undesirable wood. Apply gloss or semigloss enamel over one or more primer coats of paint to give furniture pieces tough, cleanable surfaces.

OIL, such as linseed or tung, enhances the natural appearance and grain of wood. Simply rub the oil into the surface with a clean rag. Apply several coats, wiping the excess from the surface after each application. Oil finishes are delicate but can be easily repeated to restore them.

STAIN is a colored pigment that penetrates the wood surface to alter its color. Stain generally indicates that the appearance of the finish differs from the wood type it covers.

WAX provides a protective finish for a wood surface while maintaining its natural appearance. It may darken the wood slightly and, like a tung or linseed oil finish, needs to be reapplied periodically. To bring out a sheen, buff waxed surfaces. You also can apply wax over a shellacked, varnished, or oiled finish.

Cedar. Brown to white, it often is used for drawer lining or for decorative panels. Only eastern red cedar is naturally moth-repellent. Cedar is most commonly used for outdoor furniture.

Pine (white). In past decades, because it was readily available and easy to work with, white pine was used for Early American furnituremaking. Its softness is why many of these old pieces show traces of wear. Vintage pieces are valued for the patina and reasonable cost; they're frequently also painted.

Pine (yellow). Yellow-orange and grainy, this wood does not finish well and is a poor choice for exposed wood.

COMPOSITES. These manufactured wood products have various prices and performances.

Plywood. White to tan, it is made from layers of thin sheets of wood that are glued and pressed together. Strong and resistant to warping, shrinking, and swelling, it is most often used as support.

Particleboard. Usually light to medium brown, it is made of sawdust, small wood chips, and glue or resin that have

do-it-yourself dining

meals on wheels

Think outside the box when you buy first home furniture. After all, it's time for budget-conscious creativity and experimentation. These $30 office chairs inspired a conference/dining room take on furnishing a dual-purpose studio space. A hollow-core door becomes a table when fitted with legs on wheels.

easy-chair dining

Here's a furniture equation to take to the bank: 4 easy chairs + 1 tea table + 2 TV trays + 1 lamp = all the comforts of home in one affordable room. In a single, small space, you can sit back, converse, eat, watch television, read, do office work, and gaze out a window. Store your books on a shelf under the table and move TV-tray side tables about as needed.

kitschy kitchen

After they're assembled, two 30-inch-square RTA (ready-to-assemble) tables add eat-in room in a kitchen when they're placed end-to-end against a wall. At the wall end, an RTA shoe-stacker unit stores everyday table settings and lightweight $10 folding chairs work well for seating. Someday they'll go to the closet as extra party seating when new chairs move in.

cleaning a found treasure

To renew an old table, you may need to deep-clean it to remove layers of grime. As a first step, use an oil soap and water to remove dirt. Rinse and dry well. If the finish still seems dirty, clean with #0000 steel wool dipped in naphtha or acetone. Or instead of naphtha, use a commercial wood- cleaning product. Some products with a milky appearance are formulated to dissolve solvent-based and oil-based residues. Do not use mixtures containing boiled linseed oil, turpentine, or white vinegars. They darken wood and attract dust and lint. Instead, apply clear paste wax to the table.

style on a budget

Mixing old pieces with new is easier if you choose clean lines. For example, pair old oak armchairs with contemporary wicker Parsons chairs, *opposite*. They work well together because of their simple shapes.

country in the city

A large blue and white check wallcovering brings a light, contemporary voice to this kitchen/dining room furnished with antique pine and white-painted furniture. For creative lighting, a table lamp is plugged into a wall socket to focus on the tabletop, and a string of lights draped around the window frame adds a festive note.

secondhand style

elegant cottage dining

This small dining room is a pass-through space from the living room to the kitchen. Even though it is not walled off, it implies the formality of a separate space for sit-down dinners. The once-dark red and black mahogany table from an antiques store was updated with a crackle finish in tones of cream and beige.

51

store
it with style

utility chic

For an inexpensive and handsome place to store dining room tableware, hang adjustable metal shelving units purchased at home improvement or discount home furnishings stores. Stack dishes in plain view and arrange linens and flatware in boxes and woven baskets.

Whether your home has one dining area or formal and informal dining spaces, storage in or near the dining area is the key to organization and function. Built-ins can be customized, but freestanding wardrobes, cupboards, and armoires adapt well and add style to a setting.

freestanding storage

When looking for freestanding storage, consider something other than a piece that matches your dining table and chairs. You often can find better buys on antique, vintage, reproduction, or contemporary sideboards that are sold separately. And by mixing and matching, you'll learn more about your own personal style and make purchases that help build toward your future plans.

MINI SIDEBOARD. No space for a conventional server or sideboard? Purchase a vintage or reproduction demilune (half-round) chest or other small chest. Line the drawers with silver-storage cloth to slow tarnishing if you are storing sterling or silver-plated pieces.

ROLLING CART. Convert a ready-to-assemble (RTA) outdoor bar cart into a temporary indoor storage unit. Later, when you find something better, use the cart outdoors.

CORNER CUPBOARD. Fit a compact corner cupboard into a small dining area. Look for vintage pieces or paint an unfinished one. Use its top for extra storage and display.

BUTLER'S PANTRY. Traditionally, the butler's pantry is a small room between the dining room and kitchen used for storing china, silver, glassware, serving pieces, and linens. However, many of the pantry's convenient organizing ideas also can be incorporated into dining rooms and informal dining areas. Although storage in a butler's pantry is often custom-built, stock pieces, such as plate and glass organizers and lazy Susans, can turn a closet or sideboard into your own version of this pantry.

mini butler's pantry

Convert a pie safe for dish storage that is arranged so beautifully you will want to keep the doors open. Heavy serving pieces anchor the lower shelves; for balance, three bowls stairstep across the top. Smaller pieces are stored in stacks for ready use for the table.

built-in storage

For ways to add permanent storage to your dining room, explore these built-in possibilities.

FLOOR-TO-CEILING SIDEBOARD. Turn an interior wall of your dining room into a sideboard by installing floor-to-ceiling cabinets. Use the top cabinet to store little-used or seasonal items, such as holiday decorations. This arrangement provides much-needed storage in houses without basements or attics. It also is better than garage storage for temperature and humidity control, especially in damp climates.

AROUND-THE-WINDOW STORAGE. In a small dining room, build a wall of cabinets and open shelves around the window. Include a wine rack, if desired.

BETWEEN-THE-STUDS CHINA CABINET. Find room for a built-in china cabinet by using space between wall studs. This shallow storage works for glasses and plate display.

SIDEBOARD OR SERVER. Maximize storage and function with a built-in sideboard or server for china, flatware, linens, and serving pieces. Measure your plates, trays, and serving platters for a custom fit. Add a built-in china cabinet with glass doors on both sides to define a dining area without blocking light.

GLASS SHELVES. In an informal dining area, take advantage of the counter between the kitchen and dining room by attaching glass shelves with metal supports. Glass keeps the look open and adds display spaces. If you have curved wood shelves, common in homes built in the 1940s and 1950s, replace them with glass.

quick fixes

Try these ideas for updating secondhand pieces or creating new servers by combining small items.

REPLACE SOLID DOORS with glass-paned ones to update an old server.

FINISH an old sideboard with a combination of colors or stains and updated hardware.

REPLACE PULLS on a built-in or freestanding server with fanciful shapes, such as knives and forks, stylized leaves, or animals. To stretch your dollar, mix these special pulls with plain ones from a home center. Or mix plain pulls of different colors.

COMBINE TWO metal or sturdy wood wine racks with a glass or painted plywood top for a server with storage. Place it away from direct sun to avoid damage to wine.

PURCHASE a commercial serving stand from a restaurant supply company and top it with a decorative tray to create a server.

MAKE A SIDEBOARD SERVER by skirting a plywood base and cutting a plywood top to fit it. Use a heavy cloth, such as tightly woven linen, to cover the server to the floor. Take advantage of the space underneath—with baskets, a wicker trunk, or boxes—for extra out-of-sight storage. Or buy a pair of stacked, pullout vinyl bins on stands and place them underneath to organize linens and serving pieces.

RTA storage

• **BOOKCASES**
Combine adjustable wood shelves as a wall unit to store dining needs in an open living/dining room.

• **CABINETS**
Glass-door cabinets you assemble yourself are an attractive way to store and display tableware. To reveal the contents, add interior lights that will cast a warm glow and add to the intimate atmosphere.

• **FREESTANDING SHELVING UNITS**
Store tableware on open shelving units that stand on their own. Use one as a room divider to define living and dining spaces or place it against a wall as a focal-point storage piece.

• **ROLLING CARTS**
Store your most used tabletop pieces on a rolling cart to use as a side serving table or drinks bar.

ED THE WORLD, THERE WOULD
BUT ALOT MORE POISON
AWYERS GIVE ALL THE REST
AD NAME"

THE CORNER FOR MY BLIND DATE.
IRL WALKED BY, I SAID, "ARE YOU
E SAID, "ARE YOU RICHARD?" I SAID
SAID, "I'M NOT LINDA".

Says to his doctor,
WHAT?!"

etween myself and a madman is that
I'M NOT MAD!"

Love notes? Quotable quotes? What's for lunch? A screenplay in progress? Hang a chalkboard over a dining area sideboard for personal expressions and changeable art. The serving bar, made from painted lumber, was distressed to match the salvaged antique brackets attached to the wall for its support.

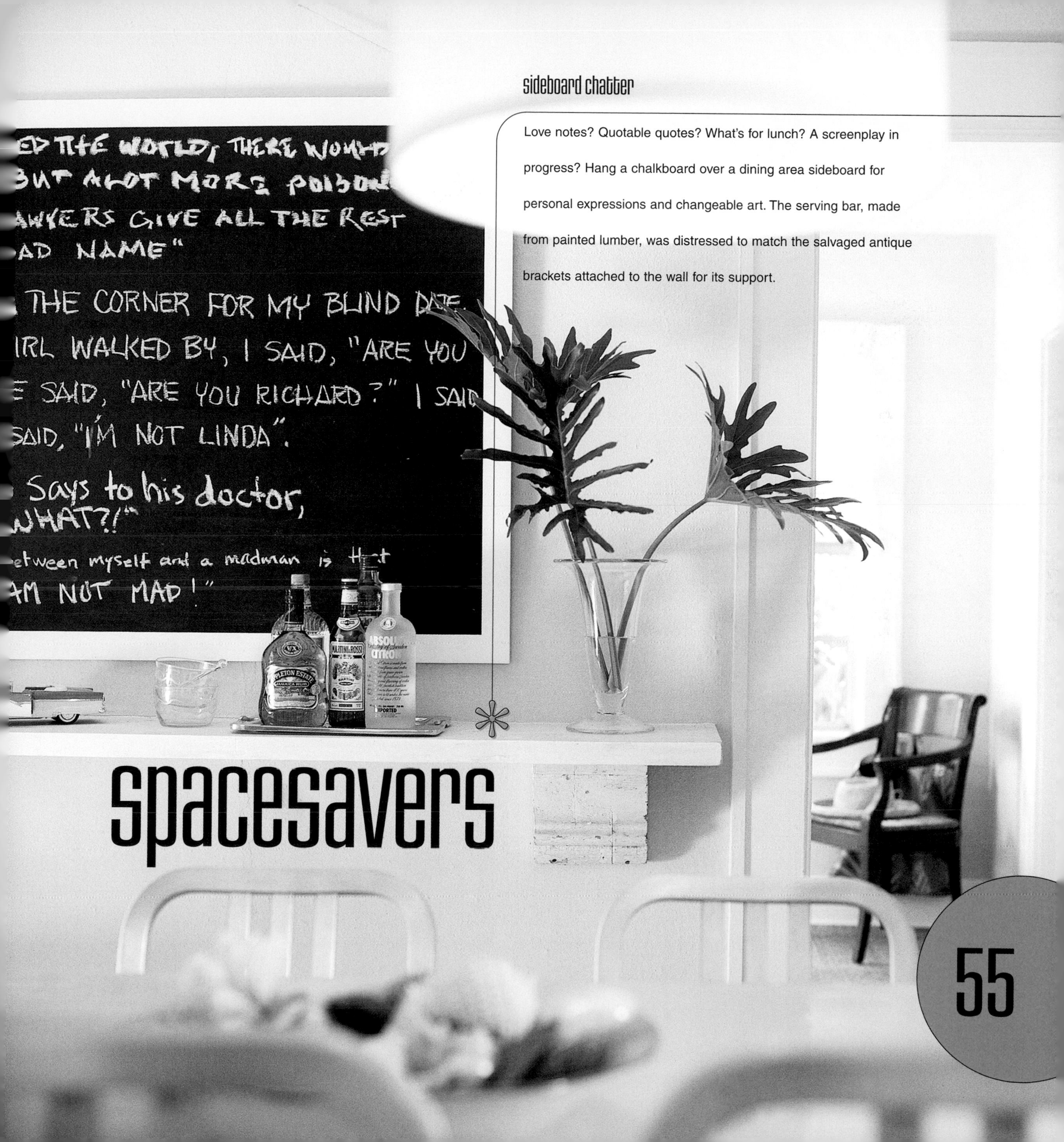

spacesavers

set **the** **table**

Think of entertaining as sharing your home and hospitality with your family and friends or as a pleasant way to turn acquaintances into friends. Entertaining also is a way to thank people for special help or to recognize noteworthy occasions.

Everyone enjoys gatherings more when they're different. Creativity, not what you spend, is the key. Special occasions—such as a Cinco de Mayo birthday party or a Bastille Day boat ride—can be the most appealing.

entertaining tips

Choose what works for you, your lifestyle, your budget, and your home. Do what is comfortable, affordable, and, most of all, fun.

KNOW YOUR LIMITS. Spend no more time and money than you can afford. Decide whether you can do everything yourself. If not, ask a friend or two to help with the preparation, errands, and cleanup. Or plan a potluck or progressive dinner, which moves from house to house, where the expense and work are shared.

BE INCLUSIVE. Casual get-togethers or backyard parties are an easy way to introduce a friend, neighbor, or coworker to others. If a family is new to your area, plan an event where children are welcome.

RECIPROCATE YOUR WAY. If you accept two or three dinner invitations or attend several parties at a person's home, you should reciprocate—if you want to continue the social relationship. This doesn't mean you must entertain the same way. A formal dinner can be returned with a casual Sunday supper. A cocktail party can be returned with a picnic in the park. If you are unable to entertain, treat your friend to a restaurant meal or a movie. The gesture and hospitality are what counts.

PERFECT PARTY MENUS AND IDEAS. Look for simple make-ahead meals, dinner salads, grilled meats, or seafood dishes that use fresh, seasonal ingredients. You may be inclined to entertain more frequently if you can make your own pretested menus and recipes with confidence and present them in your own personal style. Practice also allows for spontaneous gatherings.

MAKE A PARTY MEMORABLE. Serve a special drink, pick a theme, or celebrate the first day of spring or the longest night of the year. Other ideas: Set up a fondue potluck, make-your-own-pizza night, and wine or beer or cheese tasting party. Instead of a cocktail party, throw a chocolate and champagne party or a jazz brunch.

buffets

Use buffets in several ways: to serve a complete meal, for drinks and hors d'oeuvres only (the cocktail party), for dessert and coffee, or as an open house reception. Buffets work well because guests serve themselves and because you can accommodate a guest list larger than your dining table. Plan traffic flow and arrange your table or server (sideboard) accordingly. Stack plates, flatware, and napkins at a logical beginning point. Arrange condiments next to the dish they accompany. Don't add awkward objects such as slender candlesticks or overly large centerpieces. An edible centerpiece—a fresh fruit plate or decorated dessert tart—makes sense when dining space is tight.

If you are hosting a large party, rent the extras that you need—party chairs and tables, chafing dishes to keep food hot, and wineglasses. If guests will sit at tables, place water glasses and empty wineglasses on each table before the party. Have an open bottle of wine (or a bottle of red and a bottle of white) and a pitcher or carafe of water at each table. If guests will not be sitting at set tables—but will be sitting in the living room—arrange a separate table with drinks, glasses, and coffee service. Some hosts place desserts on this secondary table.

For an informal buffet, make the table appealing by using colorful cotton napkins, interesting serving pieces, arrangements of fruit or flowers—anything that makes the table vibrant, up-to-the-minute, and inviting. If there is no table seating for the meal, make sure guests can serve themselves, cut the food with a fork, and eat easily while sitting with a plate in their laps.

style on a budget

Switch and save. Serve guests a festive wine or champagne punch instead of wine or mixed drinks. Substitute white table wine for tequila in frozen margaritas for a change of pace.

centerpieces

For formal occasions, place centerpieces in the center of the table. If the table is quite long, use two centerpieces. Centerpieces are often fresh flowers, but fruit and vegetables may be used instead or mixed with flowers. Art objects are another possibility. Choose a centerpiece that doesn't obstruct the view of guests sitting across from each other. A soup tureen or low bowl is ideal for holding an arrangement.

For casual dinners, forget the rules—except that guests should be able to see over the centerpiece. Flowers always are appropriate—especially freshly picked blooms from your garden.

57

Generally, the less work you put into arranging flowers, the better they look.

general tips

When you purchase flowers, be sure they're wrapped so they are protected from cold winter winds or drying heat. When you get them home, remove most of the foliage from their stems and make fresh cuts on the ends of their stems so they can drink more freely. Then immerse the stems in a bucket of cold water and put the bucket in a cool spot until you are ready to make your arrangement.

Don't force flowers into unwieldy shapes. Let them tell you by their natural growth which container they want. For example, short-stemmed buds and flowers suggest generous containers. Tall, slender-stemmed flowers beg for tall, simple cylinders that will show off their forms.

arrange flowers

There are no rules about which flowers go in what vase. Any type of flower can be treated to a casual container for an informal look or dressed up for a more formal occasion. If you're a beginner at arranging flowers, mixing and matching flowers may seem daunting. For the easiest arranging methods that will get you surefire results, stick with flowers of one color or one type. The single-color bouquet or the single-flower-type bouquet is as wonderful as any mixed one.

10-minute flower arranging

Flowers cheer up a weary room, make an occasion special, and put a new spin on your outlook. For quickly assembled flower displays to fit a busy schedule, try these methods.

POSY PARADE. Arrange five water-filled drinking glasses in a straight line down the center of a table or along the back of a sideboard. Cut the stems of five lilac, hydrangea, or peony blooms slightly longer than the height of the glasses. Lean the blooms over the edges of the glasses in pleasing positions down the line.

ROSE BOWL. Pour water into a piece of stemware that has a generous, flared-out bowl. Cut the stems of six fully opened roses to about 4 inches and remove the leaves. Crowd the blooms together in the bowl and ring the mound of flowers with short stems of lemon leaves. This is an especially effective mood-maker on a small, private dinner table. Add a candle or two, and you are set for a wonderful time with someone you love.

SINGLE & LOVING IT. A single, perfect bloom standing in a tall, elegant piece of stemware will be the star attraction on your midnight buffet table. Tuck it in among your best crystal and stemware glasses so your guests can admire it as they serve themselves.

DITCH-WEED ARRANGEMENT. Search ditches for a free supply of wonderful weeds and grasses (avoid cutting in protected areas) to slip into green containers. For vases, gather great-looking olive oil, wine, and vinegar bottles to use as bud vases. Fill them with water, slip a single stem or two of nonwilting weeds or grasses into each (clip their stems as necessary), and mass the bottles on a decorative tray.

PITCHER PERFECT. In your repertoire of vases, include one tall white urn-shaped pitcher to display cuttings of May bridal wreath, apple blossoms, mustard, dill weed, daisies, and other spreading branches. The narrow neck at the top of the pitcher gathers stems together, while the broad base allows their bottoms to splay out. This assures a loose and casual arrangement that leans gracefully over the lip of the pitcher in all directions.

WATER GARDEN. Water is an essential part of flower arranging that usually is hidden inside the container. Unless your vase is glass, you miss it. A large salad bowl filled with water, stones, and a bloom or two is one way to showcase this fluid, life-giving element. This is the perfect setup for a single gardenia or rose. Float a candle to add light.

MILK CARRIER SHOWCASE. Slip a milk bottle into each section of an antique milk carrier to create an impressive floral display with just a few stems. These casual bud vases keep floppy flowers standing upright. If you have no milk carrier, use wine carafes in a sectioned-off wicker basket or soda bottles in a soda crate.

PAPER BAG VASE. It is tempting to ignore the usual flower vases when you see the colorful array of paper bags available for gift wrap. All you need is a waterproof vase that fits inside the bag out of sight. A drinking glass works well.

LOW BOWLER. For a low and wide arrangement in a bowl, use floral foam to keep flowers in place. Cut away the edges of a foam block with a paring knife until it fits snugly inside the bowl. Soak the foam in water for 30 minutes. Then insert short-stemmed flowers into the foam in a fairly even mound.

EVER GREEN. In winter, don't stop arranging. Although everything else in the garden has gone dormant, evergreens tell you there is still life on the planet. Cut fresh branches from evergreen trees, shrubs, or bushes and set them in a wide-mouthed, bucket-shaped vase filled with water. Or make a bouquet from red dogwood twigs or branches.

mastering stains

- **RED WINE, LIPSTICK.** Sponge or soak stain using cool water. Pretreat with stain remover or liquid laundry detergent. Launder with fabric-safe bleach.
- **GRAVY.** Pretreat or soak with a product containing enzymes. Soak for 30 minutes if stain is dry. Launder as usual; dry only after stain is out.
- **CANDLE WAX.** Scrape with a dull knife. If wax remains, place between paper towels and press with a warm iron. Replace towels as wax is absorbed.
- **TOMATO SAUCE, OLIVE OIL, BUTTER.** Apply a prewash stain remover or liquid laundry detergent. Wash with liquid laundry detergent, using safe bleach and safe water temperature.
- **COFFEE OR TEA.** Pretreat with stain remover or liquid laundry detergent. Or rub with bar soap. Launder as usual. Rewash if needed.

60

where you work

lord of the files

Skip the long drive and give up the cubicle. Instead—if your work style suggests it—create a space at home that cultivates your creativity and seems anything but boxed in. States away from its base operation, this Webmaster's office is the focal point, communications center, and entertainment core of a living room space.

assess
your needs

Home offices have an array of styles and functions—from a tiny bookkeeping spot at the kitchen table to an entire room devoted to a full-time occupation.

What tasks do you plan to accomplish in your home office? Does home office mean a place to pay your bills, keep records for tax purposes, and store photograph albums? Do you have a part-time, home-based occupation that requires a small office for communication and bookkeeping or a lot of storage for products? Or are you part of the legions joining the home-working revolution at your company's request or because you have chosen it?

What kind of an environment motivates your productivity? Do you prefer an officelike atmosphere far from the reminders of dirty dishes, laundry, and distracting chores of home? Or do you get inspiration from an office that reflects the style of your home and integrates its functions with the way you live?

In this chapter, you will find examples of home office and work styles, information on buying office furniture, and ideas for organizing your plans for getting down to business at home.

63

what's your work style?

PARIS

NEW YORK

DES MOINES

LOS ANGELES

part-time paper pusher

Not every job requires miles of desk space,

so choose your work surface accordingly.

Although not wide, this custom-stained desk

is deep enough to hold a generous amount

of work. To personalize a small desk and

incorporate it into a basement or family

room, buy an unfinished piece and give it a

painted finish.

Are you a stay-in-touch type with a list of clients around town or across the country? Do you need to leave home to execute sales? A home office set-up works well—even when you travel out of town on assignment. Like a homing pigeon, you return to a nest of files and furniture that keeps your work life in order and gives your daily life an overall sense of security.

high flier

Perhaps the nearest surface—the pull-down table on a plane, a hotel bed, or a restaurant table—is all the desk you usually have to accomplish your tasks. When you're home, the wide-open spaces of the dining room table may feel appealing. Although you carry information around in your head and count on your computer to back you up, you'll want paper records of your work and storage to hold them. Work them into units and files around the house.

what you need

desk
table, counter, or hollow-core door on legs

comfortable chair

storage
filing boxes, bookcases, rolling cart

lighting
overhead, task

timekeepers
clock, day planner, calendar

communication devices
telephone, e-mail, or fax; pens, pencils

paper
stationery, printer supplies, notepads, notebooks

books
resource, reference, inspirational, record keepers

large equipment
computer, printer, scanner

small equipment
calculator, stapler, scissors, cash box, tape dispenser

small storage
lidded boxes, baskets, envelopes, paper files

trash container

window shades

portable music player

mugs, cups, glasses

ice container, coffee pot

what you'll want

dream desk

dream chair

storage
built-ins custom-made to your tasks

lighting
recessed, task, novelty

upgraded computer

digital camera/photo printer

wall art

built-in kitchen
microwave, refrigerator, cooktop, sink

personal entertainment center
DVD player, television, CD player, AM/FM radio, and clock

window treatments
venetian blinds or plantation shutters

client table & chairs

paper shredder

message, memo, or bulletin board

portable desktop fan

digital tape recorder

massage chair

plan
your space

Tuck a tiny office into a corner of your bedroom by outfitting a painted clothing armoire with a computer shelf and keyboard tray.

command central

Swivel about in a concentrated work space on a floor surface that allows easy movement. Wood laminate flooring is a good choice for mobility. A thin berber carpet does the same while reducing noise. For beauty's sake, slipcover an ergonomic, utilitarian chair.

pick a spot

What is your work style, and what are your aims? Are you looking for a work space away from the hubbub of home life? Do you plan to make your office the heart of your home and integrate your lifestyle with your work? Or do you want a balance between these two extremes?

DINING ROOM. A little-used dining room works well for work during the week. With good storage, you can clear it easily for weekend entertaining.

EXTRA BEDROOM. A walk-through bedroom with doors on both sides works well as a grand-central home office/homework station. A guest room with a pullout sleeper is another option.

CORNERS & CLOSETS. If you can't spare a room for an office, convert an awkward corner on a landing, under the stairs, or in a closet. A closet under a stairwell holds potential for deep storage of seldom-used files, and the forward section promises space for a worktop.

ATTIC, BASEMENT, OR GARAGE. Convert one of these spaces if you have the funds.

Plan your ideal office on paper, including furniture, storage, and lighting. Then work with what you have now to get started.

get wired

Do you need power to run a computer, printer, or fax? If so, supply them with their own electrical circuit maintained by a surge protector. If you have an older home, ask an electrician to see whether you should rewire.

a surface that works

Work begins with an inviting surface, which, for you, may not mean a formal desk. Choose the worktop that suits you and your work style best—just be sure it's the right size and height for your tasks. A standard writing surface is about 30 inches tall, while a comfortable keyboard height is 26 inches.

FREESTANDING DESK OR TABLE. A sturdy table—a dining room table, a hollow-core door set on castered legs, or a foldout worktop—may be all you need to get productive. If you can't live without access to drawers at your side, invest in a formal desk or rolling file cabinets. Or make your own desk with storage by using two contemporary-style filing cabinets to support a glass top. (Make sure the edges are beveled for safety.) Use the files for storing your worktop needs.

COMPUTER UNIT OR DESK. Shop office supply stores for an inexpensive computer workstation. You'll find many options. Wheeled versions offer mobility, and some have adjustable work-surface heights.

BUILT-IN WORKTOP. Consider desk space with shelves and storage to optimize space.

a feel-good chair

Comfort in a home office is key. Choose a chair that alleviates your body's stress from sitting for hours in the same spot. An adjustable chair with a five-point base offers flexibility and stability. Unless you plan to sit in your chair for only short periods, choose a chair with allover padding and adjustable angles and heights. Give the chair a good test. When you lean forward or back, does it support your spine? Is good posture natural and easy? Does the chair back give extra support to the lumbar region of your spine? If you buy a chair with adjustable armrests (expensive but worth it), look for armrests that keep your arms parallel to the floor. For easy movement and turnaround power in your work space, buy a chair equipped with wheels and a swivel mechanism.

storage that stands up

Make an inventory of office items you need to store and then consider the following options:

SHELVES. They work best for storing reference books and items you need to keep in view. Ready-to-assemble shelf units stand as high as you like and move easily about when you decide to rearrange your office. Built-ins make the best use of space but are difficult to change once they are established on walls. Home center cabinetry may save you money.

CLOSED CABINETS. An armoire, filing cabinet, or chest of drawers hides unattractive items such as hanging folders, box and ring files, storage cases, and CDs.

WALL POCKETS & BOX FILES. Keep small papers in check and at arm's length with an array of attractive, matching containers. Roll large papers into cylinders and stand them in tall laundry or wastebaskets.

 # mini offices

IN THE CLOSET
• Hang double bifold doors for accessibility.
• Outfit the closet with a drawing board for a work surface, upper shelves, a lower bin with pullout baskets, and a filing cabinet.
• Stock the upper shelves with see-through plastic boxes or bins for easy reference.
• Hang a bulletin board, pegboard, racks, or other wall-mounted storage on the side walls to organize tools or office supplies.

ON WHEELS
If space is tight, stock a small supply cart on wheels to roll in and out of a closet.

70

Get more function out of your work surface. Turn it into an impromptu dining table for a business lunch with clients. Keep office-style tableware handy in a nearby cabinet or cupboard.

choose furniture

heavy metal

This antique mail-sorting station from a Paris flea market finds new life in America as a gardener's billing station. To give your work space a style reflecting your personality, shop for furniture in antiques and secondhand stores or at architectural salvage companies. Look for office potential in pieces intended for schools or stores.

A poorly lit office cuts your productivity, zaps your spirit, and leaves you wondering why you feel like a slug.

daylight

Sunlight has the power to lift spirits and get you riding the work wave. The ideal location for your desk or your computer screen is at a right angle to a window. If you have no such option, swivel your screen to avoid glare and control the sun with window treatments. Soft blinds, sheers, curtains, and shades suit an office occupant with traditional tastes. For bring-it-on professional types, venetian blinds and wooden shutters with flexible blades or slats are ideal for light control.

artificial light

Even if you don't work, you need overhead and task lighting in your home office.

OVERHEAD lighting illuminates a room in a general way, showing you where large objects are and where you can walk without bumping into things. During daylight, artificial light isn't necessary if you make good use of the natural light that comes in through your doors, windows, and window treatments. At night, a row of hanging fixtures, recessed lighting, or a ceiling fixture takes over the function of daylight.

TASK lighting aims directly at your work. Experiment with brightness and flexibility until you find the right level. For short stints at your desk, you can get by with a spare household tabletop lamp, but if you spend many hours in the same spot, get a lamp designed for your specific work purposes.

instant office

In the blink of an eye, a lightweight worktop, swivel chair, and wheel-around storage unit create an office anywhere in the house. When you want to move it, you can quickly set up shop in another room.

Desk or table lamps suit traditional offices. More flexible than any other light, they require no installation. Simply plug them in and turn them on—but pay attention to their height, light, and style. Before you go lamp shopping, measure the height of your desk, then take along a tape rule to measure each lamp from its base to the bottom of the shade. You want the combined height of these two measurements to be around 40 inches (seated eye level). The best buy is a lamp with a flexible neck or a swinging arm you can adjust.

Clamp lights, which are available in varying degrees of flexibility and in various styles, work like table lamps.

Undercabinet lights reduce eyestrain and lend a professional ambience to your work space. Is there a shelf in front of your work surface? Attach a light strip on its underside and conceal the strip behind a decorative edging applied at the front of the shelf.

style on a budget

Make a lamp from a home improvement center lamp kit and a lamp base from almost anything–a teapot, a wine-making jug, a clay pot, or an interesting chunk of wood.

box office

Turn an unfinished television and entertainment storage unit into an office by planning its interior for the best use in your work space; paint it with colors that fit the room. Install the shelving that came with the unit. Top with a ready-to-assemble closet unit made for 15 pairs of shoes. Forget the shoes—use the cubbies for small items you need now and then.

organize
your stuff

identical files

Line open shelves in around-the-window built-in storage shelves

with magazine files, photo boxes, and new 1-gallon paint cans.

Label each container to keep everything at your fingertips.

zoning laws

- **ZONE #1: DESKTOP**
Prime space is within 24 to 30 inches of your desk
top. Assign this area to frequently used essentials.
- **ZONE #2: CHAIR SWIVEL SPACE**
Secondary space, a moderate distance from the
desktop, goes to supplies and materials that are used
frequently but not every day.
- **ZONE #3: GET-UP-FROM-YOUR-CHAIR SPACE**
A final zone, which can be in another room if space is
tight, can go to rarely used files and books. Purchase
a cart on wheels from an office supply store and roll it
out as needed; store it in a closet.

A well-organized storage system gets you operating efficiently in a calm and orderly atmosphere.

don't sweat the small stuff

Add plastic bins and storage boxes from home organizing and discount stores. Use flowerpots or decorative woven baskets to hold pens, pencils, and scissors.
DESK DRAWERS. Organize with plastic divider trays or boxes to store pens, paper, paper clips, tape, and stamps. Use file folders to keep papers neat and organized.
OPEN STORAGE. Organize with matching metal record bins available from shops and catalogs that specialize in storage solutions. Check discount stores too.

Substitute flat baskets for "in" and "out" boxes. Use larger baskets for mail, magazines, and projects. Add baskets with handles, including the divided baskets designed for buffet flatware.
OPEN SHELVES. Conceal less-than-decorative items on open shelves by storing them inside wicker attaché cases, baskets with tops, or well-made picnic baskets.
TRUNKS & BINS. Use vintage suitcases, wicker trunks, and blanket bins to store larger items. They are ideal under work counters or desks. Visit import or specialty gift stores for out-of-the-ordinary options. Footed boxes, stacked bandboxes, and small leather trunks neatly hold office supplies.

the personal factor

Create an atmosphere for a good output of work by organizing a serene office space free of diversions.

COLOR & PATTERN. Choose solid colors for walls. Green, the color of tranquillity, is an ideal office choice. Gray encourages passivity while yellow and orange bring out your confidence. Blue can be as uplifting as a clear sky or as cold as ice, depending on its lightness or darkness or your sensitivity to it. Red offers positive energy and strength; too much of it makes some people angry or exhausted. Warm a too-cool white space with cream or another neutral. Overall, vary the decorating enough so that a single color doesn't bring on monotony or leave you feeling too uninspired to work.

FURNITURE ARRANGING. The ideal desk placement is opposite the door with your chair facing the door. Leave a space at your back between you and the wall for free movement and good air circulation. Placing your desk with your back to the door or facing a wall leaves you vulnerable to surprises. If those arrangements are the only possibilities, hang a mirror on the wall so you can view the door and avoid jumping out of your skin when someone suddenly enters. Keep your desk clear of messes that will confuse and distract you. To avoid working in your shadow, place your task light on the opposite side of your writing hand.

ORIGINALLY YOURS. Your personal style will naturally fall into place when you choose the furnishings for your office. Extend your style into the small work accessories by selecting objects that appeal to your senses and keep you interested in coming back to work. For example, if a particular style of calculator appeals to you, indulge yourself in the purchase. Does music put you in a productive mode? If so, invest in a DVD player, CD player, or stereo system; add a library of soundtracks that inspire you.

cubism, circa now

In a small office shared by two, chaos might be king. Organize the space with cubes of storage that hide bits and pieces that could distract the eye and keep it from focusing on a task. A work surface custom-built for two, this partners' desk takes on a variety of tasks, depending on whether you're working at the computer, making jewelry, or painting pictures.

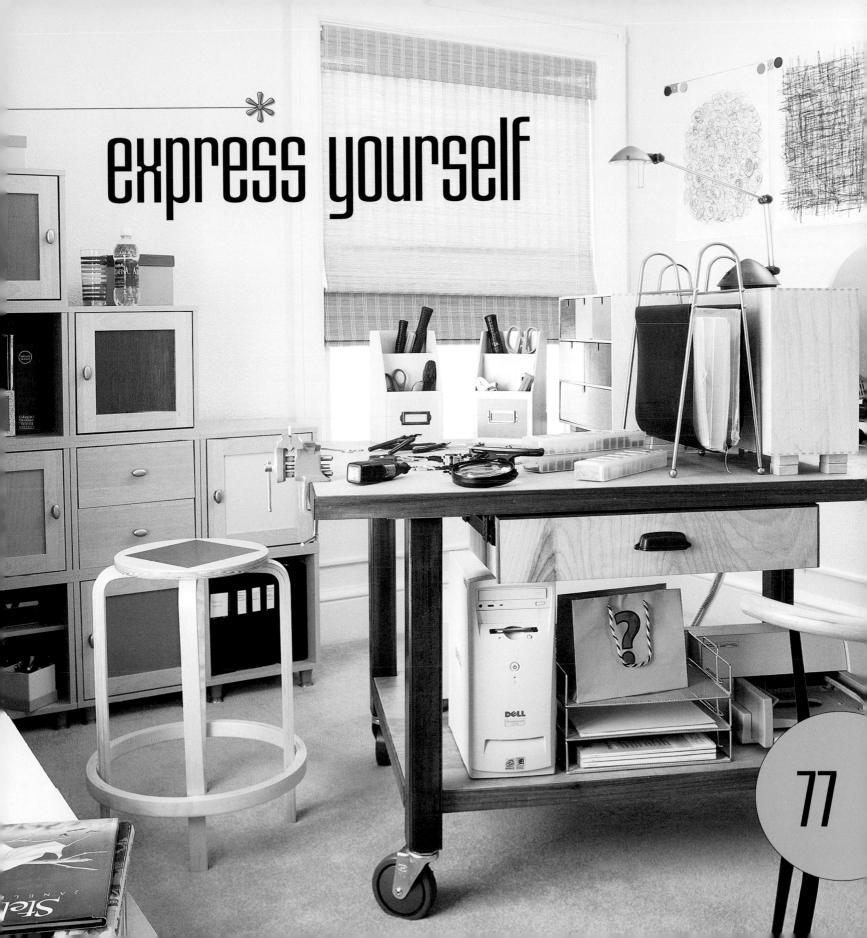

express yourself

where you

relax

Think of your living space as a theater, where life plays out in the company of your fans. The best seats are reserved for you and those who love you the most.

If your living room were a movie set, would it resemble Audrey Hepburn's low-fat flat in *Breakfast at Tiffany's*? Johnny Depp's *Chocolat* houseboat? Sandra Bullock's Victorian manse in *Practical Magic*? Or would it look more like Amelie's touchy-feely cocoon? Austin Powers' shagadelic pad?

OK, so you play house for real. You star in the adventures of your own story and live out the spare moments of your life, relaxing in a space only you know how to design. Setting up a relaxation space is your big chance to organize living as you see it. Fill the most public room in your house with the furnishings that express your style and comfortably fit the gang that hangs out with you.

Does your new home have a formal living room as well as an informal kitchen/family room? A spacious great-room? A cozy den? Or do you expect one single space to fulfill all your fun functions, such as vegging, viewing, entertaining, or working the phone? In this chapter you'll find inspiration and information that will help you design a room where you can live a larger-than-life-size life.

APARTMENT *for* RENT
FURNISHED

some like it hot

Call it the wow factor—a hit with some crowds. When you choose a bright, bold room, you are a creative type—an emotional exhibitionist—open to the world. You go through various phases that show up in your living spaces. For you, nothing is forever in decorating. Have fun but remember that comfort and function are the bones of good design.

set the scene

are you a master of the mix?

Do you get decorating thrills from mixing modern with traditional? If so, you like creating a dialogue between old and new, which can lead to some quirky moments. If loose pages fall out of a $10 book of bird prints, you might yank the rest out for a wall display above a Victorian fainting couch you covered with orange crushed velvet.

what's your style?

82

mad for mod?

The soul of modernity thrives on functional, no-frills furniture. Push modular square tables together or pull them apart as needed—perfect if your living room doubles as a dining room. This buffet is two sofa tables covered with a tablecloth. Cube ottomans provide flexible seating.

calm & collecting?

Home is a treasure chest when you're a collector. Like a connoisseur of wine, you enjoy life one sip at a time. You probably are faithful to one color—light and dark variations of taupe or beige, for example—but flirt with texture. You paint the walls cream-white, band your windows with light-filtering shades, and show off your collection of white bowls and pottery on antique pine cabinets and shelves. Wicker-y Parsons chairs pulled up around a tiny ottoman let you enjoy the afternoon light and share a glass of wine with a friend.

are you quirky—as in liberace meets a paris flea market?

If this picture resembles your style, you're not shy about picking a color palette. You try Chinese red in the kitchen, Tiffany-box blue in the bedroom, fuchsia in the hallway—it's only paint. You shop obsessively but wisely. Unlike paint, furniture mistakes aren't easily rectified, and you don't commit unless you are absolutely in love. You choose one drop-dead piece and build your look around it—maybe a French living room chair or killer Indian fabrics.

genteel with a french accent?

Never mind that practically nothing you own comes from France. It's the look that counts. You develop character with interesting furniture and fabrics. You show curves—a half-round, or demilune, chest is classic French style, a sassy 1940s chair has French Deco influences, and cabriole legs on a round table chair whisper francais. Above all, you have flair. Like all French gentry, you are born with a gift for accessorizing— subtle, not gauche.

85

what you need

starter sofa
upholstered old or new, futon/mattress, or wicker/cushions

starter armchairs
secondhand or new

storage
do-it-yourself ledges, shelving, rolling cart, baskets

lighting
overhead, floor lamp, or table lamp

tables
coffee, cube, nesting, pedestal, or half-round

casual toss pillows

casual throws

flower vases

candleholders

candles

basic window treatments
shades, blinds, or sheers

casual floor covering
area rug or runner, carpet, or design painted on the floor

artwork

what you'll want

dream sofa
high quality, custom covered, or designer classic

dream armchairs
upholstered classics; leather reclining

designer classic side chair as art

upscale storage
sideboard, armoire, or entertainment unit

flat-screen television

original paintings

artful flower vases

handcrafted art pieces

bookshelves

stereo system

VCR/DVD player

luxury pillows, throws

decorative window treatment
fabric curtain panels hung over shades

lighting
chandelier, recessed, wall-washers, accent, or designer lamps

built-in vacuum cleaner system

plan a living space

soft and easy does it

Thrift-shop furniture and fabric, bought by the bolt from sale tables, form the basis for this relaxed style. To get the look, stick to cream-colored or white paint and pattern-free or geometric textiles.

home on the stage

A live theater production requires a backdrop, furniture, and props. To create a theater for living, plan to produce the same three layers.

IMAGINE A BACKDROP. The best background for living is one that won't steal the show from the characters moving about in it. Do you look gorgeous surrounded by peaches-and-cream walls, or does your zany personality demand vibrant colors? If you share the limelight with another, create a color compromise that suits you both.

Window dressing. The best treatments are casual, carefree fabrics that simply let in the light, and don't scream for attention or cost too much of your hard-earned cash.

Walls, floor, & ceiling. Your taste in color comes to light on your walls with paint, wallcovering, or architectural moldings you apply. Is your flooring what you want, or is stripping it of carpet the next thing you will do? Look at your fifth wall, the ceiling. Does it need painting, new lighting, or some other kind of attention?

BLOCK THE SCENE. Inventory your furniture pieces. Cut each piece from gridded paper and arrange it on a floor plan of your living room. Are they the ones you want for comfortably playing out your scenes? Do you have a sofa for parking in front of the bigscreen TV or seating for the gang to gather for cards and cocktails? Do you long for a backgammon table, an entertainment unit, or a bigger coffee table?

Sofas & chairs. A sofa is a natural for watching TV or napping but not a given if you are prone to gathering friends around a table. Four easy chairs and a round table work as well as the ubiquitous sofa and two chairs set in a U around a coffee table.

Coffee table. When a coffee table is the hub of your living space, make it larger than life. The standard proportion for a coffee table is one-half to two-thirds the length of the sofa it accompanies—go for the larger one, especially if it has shelves for storage below. Leave 14 to 18 inches of space between it and your seating pieces for passage and legroom; keep it close enough to the seating so the table does not seem to float in an open space.

Side tables. Round pedestal tables for lamps, accessories, and beverages work well as side tables between chairs and sofas. When space is tight, nesting tables pull out as needed. Vintage suitcases stack up for side tables; use the interiors for storage.

Storage. Do you have the storage for everything in your relaxation space? Do you scatter the bits and pieces of audiovisual equipment around the room on boxes, shelves, and the floor? If so, imagine a focal-point storage piece to organize everything in one place.

PROP IT. Small properties (props), such as lamps, books, trays, pillows, flowers, and candles, bring your theater set to life. Useful as they are, they also carry connotations of your personal style, simply by the way you choose and arrange them in the room.

Lighting. Although lighting may be the last thing on your list of things to do, keep it in mind. As in the theater, the show can't go on without it.

starter sofa

You have an excellent chance of finding an old sofa in your parents' basement or at a thrift store.

• **THE BIG QUESTION:** Is the sofa worth reupholstering? Given that you like the style, reupholstering is a deal if the seating system is eight-way hand-tied. To check, reach underneath; you'll feel the dust cloth. If you can't push the dust cloth up, it's because you are hitting the webbing used in hand-tied seats—a good sign. Even if the seat springs need retying or the cushions need replacing, go for it. Redoing a sofa costs $600 to $1,500. So if you buy a hand-tied, thrift-store sofa for $50 and spend $800 on reupholstering, you might end up with a better one than what you could buy new for $1,200.

• **TIP:** To be sure the upholstery fabric is right for your sofa, consult an upholsterer or purchase the fabric from him or her.

Seek the best value in upholstery by balancing the quality of the fabric with the inside construction. Remember the adage "Beauty is only skin deep"? Unless good structure and real value lie underneath, the relationship won't last. Go for budget/budget or good/good qualities—it is unwise to mix. Sit on each piece you consider. Move around. Try different positions. Do the height and depth of the seat fit the length of your legs? Can you lean back comfortably? Can you easily get in and out of the seat? Are the arms of the sofa at a comfortable height?

hey, couch potato

Sofas are big and expensive, and you have to look at them day in, day out. Are you having trouble committing? The key to picking the right sofa is a candid assessment of your lifestyle.

USE. If you watch a lot of TV, go for pillowy comfort over high style. If you are child-free and party-prone, you might choose a style that's more streamlined and won't swallow your guests.

MESSINESS. Cat hair and sticky little fingers often necessitate a fabric with a stain-disguising pattern or texture. Textured weaves and subtle color changes help hide dirt and soil. Flat finishes show spots that a tweed can hide. Plush and napped fabrics show water spots and crush with wear, resulting in a mottled, discolored appearance.

FAMILY SIZE. Seat systems break down the more a sofa or occasional chair is used. If you have six wild children and you want a 20-year sofa, pop for the pricey eight-way hand-tied variety.

STYLE FICKLENESS. If you love English country and always will, then invest in a sofa that will last 30 years. If you are an interior-design fashion slave, consider paying less for one that will wear out in about eight years.

sofa, so good

Kick the tires. Here's how much mileage you can expect from your sofa, based on average use.

BUDGET ($300–500): An inexpensive sofa lasts approximately 3 to 5 years; springs and cushions will degrade at about the same rate. The construction is a zigzag spring seat, softwood or plywood frame, and a low-price fabric.

DECENT ($800–1,200). A midrange purchase lasts 5 to 15 years; replace the cushions after 5 years. It is sure to have a hardwood frame, better zigzag spring seat, and a higher grade of fabric.

QUALITY ($1,500–2,000). This higher-end purchase lasts 25 to 30 years. Replace the cushions after 15 to 20 years. An investment sofa will have a well-constructed hardwood frame, eight-way hand-tied seating, and latex foam or spring cushions, often encased in down for added comfort.

HEIRLOOM ($2,500 AND UP). A high-end purchase lasts 35 to 65 years; replace cushions after 35. The manufacturers use the highest-quality construction methods with a fabric grade to match.

buy a sofa and chairs

fabric softener

Afraid of sand, melted crayons, or kids spilling chocolate milk on your brand-new upholstery? Cover your investment with protective slipcovers that extend the life of upholstery fabric. White cotton canvas slipcovers can go in the wash and be popped back on again without ironing.

91

more about upholstery

going to the dogs

This is not something you want to talk about in

polite company, but dogs sometimes do things on

sofas and chairs that you wish they didn't. In such

cases, loose covers are lifesavers because you can

remove them and have them dry-cleaned. This

sofa's casual style—the loose-fitting cover, the skirt,

lots of loose-back pillows, and fat rolled arms—

makes it pet- and people-friendly.

the inside story

Before going out to buy a sofa, arm yourself with these what-to-look-for tips as you check out the options.

FRAME. Hardwood such as oak makes the most durable frame, but semi-hardwoods in 1¼- to 1½-inch dimensions are good too. Low-quality frames are constructed from softwoods or plywood. Good sofas use dowels at the joints; cheap ones do not. Frames should have glue, screws (or staples), and corner blocks, and every surface of the frame should be padded to make the upholstery fabric last longer. Avoid a sofa that lets you feel wood anywhere—even on the outside back.

SEATING SYSTEM. The most telling clue about a sofa's quality is the construction of the seating system. Two kinds are available: eight-way hand-tied or zigzag springs. Zigzag springs also are known as sinuous springs and are commonly referred to by the brand name "No Sag." The worst hand-tied sofa is better than the best zigzag sofa. But zigzag sofas are not necessarily bad—the quality of the production varies. You can't judge the quality by looking at it, and the salesperson may couch a pitch in terms that sell rather than educate. The best way to tell is by sitting. A bad zigzag seat caves in when you sit on it. Over time, the springs will weaken (particularly if your linebacker buddy sits in the same spot night after night), leaving you with an upholstered sinkhole. A good zigzag seat maintains its arch. Eight-way hand-tied spring construction has the most resiliency. In this construction, coil springs are each tied with cording to surrounding springs and the frame.

SEATS, CUSHIONS, AND BACKS. Many large sofas have removable seat and back cushions.

In high-quality sofas, seat cushions are made from individually pocketed coil springs or from latex foam. The springs generally are covered with plain fabric, then wrapped with polyester batting, a layer of polyurethane foam, a plain muslin cover, and the decorative cover. These cushions are durable and unlikely to lose their shape. However, they tend to be firm, so the snuggle-in factor may be low. Unless cushions are wrapped in down, they won't cuddle up.

More common (and more affordable) are cushions made of a solid piece of polyurethane foam covered in polyester batting. A muslin cover is sewn over the cushion; then the decorative cover zips on. As long as high-quality materials are used, these cushions will last for years. The density of the foam and the amount of batting determine firmness.

take a break

At 88 inches long, this sofa sprawls. The Parsons-style arms also take up the least amount of space from the inside seating area. Although you may look a mess while napping, a modern sofa style with loose back pillows that are boxed (sewn the same way as the seat cushions with a boxing strip of fabric connecting the top and bottom pieces) always looks neat. Welting and buttons add crisp details and keep the padding in line.

assemble
storage

shelf life

Before purchasing shelving or storage units with shelves, keep these tips in mind:

Check tall pieces for stability. If a unit is top-heavy, it is more likely to topple over when filled with books and heavy objects. Some shelves and armoires have adjustable feet to compensate for uneven floors. Without them, adjust the feet with shims. Some large pieces have hidden casters, making them easy to move.

Check movable shelves to be sure they are tight and secure but still slide in and out with ease. Thin wires or tiny plastic clips will not support the weight of books for long. The most stable storage unit has a back that is securely attached and does not bow. Thin wood or cardboard backing is a sign of lesser quality.

Look for drawers in storage units that slide in and out evenly and easily. Drawers with rollers and glides on each side are best, but one center bottom roller and glide is satisfactory if the drawer won't get heavy use. A pull on each side of the drawer front (as opposed to a single center pull) also helps drawers slide evenly. Be sure the drawers have stops so they cannot be accidentally pulled all the way out. Dust liners that form a divider between each drawer usually are found only on the highest quality furniture. Drawers often are finished only on the front or for a few inches on the sides. This is not necessarily a sign of poor quality, although the highest quality drawers will be completely finished.

steal this look

Add storage that doubles as architecture in a featureless white box of a living space. Choose a focal-point wall, measure its height and width, and go shopping. This unit = 2 CD towers + 3 bookcase units. Create it from inexpensive ready-to-assemble knockdowns.

Convert a vintage armoire or wardrobe into a liquor cabinet. Reinforce shelves to store heavy bottles. Attach undershelf track-style hangers designed for footed glasses; fill flat baskets with small barkeeping needs.

how gorgeous is this?

Buy your display pieces ready-made and painted or stained. Home decorating catalogs sell shelves and brackets, including ledges for art. Stack shelves floor to ceiling for the vertical display you need. To organize a collection of small objects, buy a ready-made wall-mounted cabinet or a hanging corner cupboard.

strut your stuff

hide your stuff

storage rx

Are you sick of all your stuff scattered about?

A SHOT IN THE ARMOIRE. Adapt vintage, secondhand, or reproduction wardrobes as television cabinets. Measure your television, including its depth; some storage pieces are too shallow to hold a television. Expect to drill out the back of the unit for wiring or cut it for a better fit. Plan to add well-supported shelves. These units usually are large enough to house other entertainment equipment, as well.

REVITALIZE A ROLLING TV CART. Make an entertainment center by pairing your college-dorm wheel-around TV base with a vertical bookcase (choose one in the same wood or metal material as the cart).

BAR ON WHEELS. A butler's tray is a classic solution for working a bar into a living room; pour liquors or sherry into decanters. Vintage tea carts or metal utility carts can serve as bars that move around for a party.

CURES FOR THE BOOK-OBSESSED. Turn a closet into a library by removing the door, replacing the trim, and adding shelves. Another option: Measure a love seat or sofa and have shelves built on each side for a recessed nook. Or, if you're good with a hammer and saw and have 8-foot ceilings, build a bookshelf over a door. The same idea can work with wide cased door openings if you reinforce the spans every 24 inches. Build shelving from floor to ceiling on the unbroken wall of a family room.

MAGAZINE PRESCRIPTIONS. Purchase large flat baskets to store magazines and newspapers. If reading material takes over your living area, add one or more magazine racks. Stack magazines in flat baskets under a console table behind a sofa or against the wall or store papers in square wicker baskets or trunks with tops. Add a shelf around the perimeter of your room for basket or bin storage. Purchase metal, European-style magazine bins and attach them to the wall.

cinema therapy

That big black screen you love to look at so much is a decorating eyesore when it's turned off. When not in use, hide it behind closed doors. For a Key Largo look, fit the front of an armoire with dramatic weather-beaten shutters.

storage 101

See things for what they aren't. Here a metal
storage trunk serving as a coffee table could just as
easily be working as a bookmobile. A little library on
wheels, it can be rolled around to the side of your
reading chair or pushed into the room as a table.
(You can stack up quite a few oversize volumes
and still move it around.)

PLATO THE REPUBLIC AND OTHER WORKS

JAMES A. AUTRY LOVE & PROFIT

YOKO ONO   IMPRESSIONS   BERGEN KUNSTMUSEUM

CHIC SIMPLE   B O D Y   KNOPF

Better Homes and Gardens₀ THE NEW DECORATING BOOK   Meredith₀

white hot

tricia guild

TRADITIONAL HOME   SIGNATURE STYLE   Meredith BOOKS

stash your trash

Boxes with squared-off shapes add structure to an interior, and they're great for corralling your stuff. Check import and discount stores for picnic baskets or flea markets for small valises, old cigar boxes, toolboxes, or even beat-up lunch pails. They'll lend character to a room while they are stowing.

manage your assets

When faced with all the exotic baskets available, you may end up with interestingly shaped containers that don't meet your storage needs. Know what you need to store before visiting the import store or ordering from a catalog. Match the sizes and shapes of your containers to the items you intend them to contain.

toe the line

Paint a vertical band as a backdrop for "paintings." Mark the width of the band on the wall with small pencil marks. Working up and down from each mark with a level, lightly draw the edges of the band using the straight edge of the level. Mask off the edges (see the tip box, *opposite*) and paint. To create the paintings, take apart record album frames and paint the backs with interior paint. When the paint is dry, reassemble the frames and hang them over the vertical band.

paint and save

shock and awe

These novel approaches to painting accent walls guarantee that you will hear, "Wow, that's awesome!"

TAKE A SHINE to a dark-painted living room accent wall with silver-leaf squares (available at crafts and hobbies stores) mounted at wide intervals. Planning is the most important part of this project.

Step one. Paint one focal-point wall with a dazzling color. For drama, choose a fairly strong one, such as a Matisse blue or a Renoir red.

Step two. Plan the placement of the 4-inch squares of silver leaf. Measure the width and height of the wall. Divide the measurements into equal parts to make even intervals about 20–24 inches from side to side and top to bottom (don't plan to apply silver squares at the edges of the sides, floor, or ceiling). On the wall, mark the center of each square's position with light pencil, then measure out 2 inches in all directions to establish the perimeters of the 4-inch-square placements (use a level to be sure your lines are plumb).

Step three. Apply the silver-leaf squares using the instructions that come with the packet and silver-leaf adhesive. Tip: To avoid distressing the fragile squares of silver leaf as you rub them onto the wall, place waxed paper between the silver leaf and your fingers.

BLOCK A WALL with color in one of these five ways:

Accent wall. Paint one wall in a stunning, daring color to act as a focal-point wall in your living room. Mask off the trim and edges of the adjacent walls with painter's tape (see masking rules, *right*).

Partial accent wall. Paint a contrasting color on the wall from the floor up to a line that falls 24 inches below the ceiling. It will resemble a wainscot.

Big band. On a windowless wall, paint a one-color accent band from the floor to the ceiling (see the photograph, *opposite*). Or do a two-color band by painting a light-colored band on the wall first. Allow it to dry for two days. Then tape off a second, narrower band over the first one and paint it a darker color.

Two-color accent wall. Repeat a color band in different widths on a plain-colored wall. Choose between vertical or horizontal bands.

Gridded wall. On a white wall, lay painter's tape horizontally and vertically at 20-inch intervals. Be sure both edges of the tape are securely fastened to the wall to keep the paint from bleeding under its edges. Paint a contrasting color (or more, if you dare) in the open areas. Remove the painter's tape to reveal the blocks of color.

HOT SHOT. Paint an accent wall with a brilliant color and trim it with bands of white-hot trimwork. This adds architecture to a featureless room and showcases the brilliant color on the wall like a frame shows off a painting. For an example, see page 74.

Step one. In a white-painted room, paint a contrasting color on an accent wall from the base molding to a horizontal line 24 inches below the ceiling.

Step two. Apply white-painted wood moldings over the paint. For the horizontal band at the top, cut and fit undercap molding over the line (drill pilot holes for nails to prevent the molding from splitting). Nail straight through the molding with finishing nails. Top the undercap molding with a length of doorstop. For vertical moldings, attach screen molding strips to the wall with wood glue and nail brads, spacing them 24 inches apart.

masking rules

Painter's low-tack masking tape is king when it comes to top tools for specialty painting. Use the technique of "masking off" to avoid getting paint on areas where you don't want it.

• **TRIM AND WOODWORK**

Lay painter's tape along the edges of moldings around floors, ceilings, doors, windows, and wainscots (dados) next to the wall you plan to paint. Smooth the edge of the tape with your finger where the wall meets the trim to be sure it is well-adhered to the trim; leave the opposite edge free for easy removal.

• **DECORATIVE PAINTING**

Lay painter's tape along the outer edges of the area you plan to paint. Smooth the edge along your pencil line with your finger to be sure it is well-adhered and paint won't bleed underneath it. Leave the opposite edge of the tape loosely adhered for easy removal. Remove the tape while the paint is wet.

Put yourself and your crowd in the best light. Do it with three types of lighting:

ambient

Overhead or general lighting may not dispense enough light for individual tasks, but you need sufficient brightness to support the room's activities—playing games, watching television, reading, or checking e-mail. Match the fixture style to the room's architectural style rather than to the furniture style. For example, unless it is a quirky antique chandelier destined to be a theme maker for a funky relaxation space, the central light in your living space should not be a focal point.

When purchasing an overhead light, check the wattage of the current light. If it provides adequate light, pick a replacement fixture that emits about the same amount. If the room always has seemed dark, use a higher-wattage light and install a dimmer switch to regulate it for lower levels. In a large or long room, you may need more than one ceiling light.

task

Ambient lighting does not cover the entire room, so table and floor lamps usually provide additional light. Task lighting casts light in specific areas for certain jobs. Soft white bulbs are better than clear or colored ones. If you experience glare from the lamp, the wattage is too high. A three-way bulb or a light controlled by a dimmer switch adjusts the level.

For the most comfort, place a table lamp so that the bottom of the shade is approximately at eye level. When the shade is higher, the glare causes eyestrain; a lower lamp sheds light onto the table instead of your reading.

Keep a table lamp in proportion to the table on which it sits. The shade should be approximately two-thirds the height of the lamp base, deep enough so that a small portion of the neck (the fitting between the lamp and socket) is visible, and about $1\frac{1}{2}$ times the width of the lamp base. Some retailers code lamps and shades to make mixing and matching shades easier.

accent

Specialty lighting draws attention to a highlight of the room, such as art. Recessed spotlights and track lights are the most common accent lights, but sconces, uplights, decorative spotlights, and some table and floor lamps also can provide accent light.

SPOTLIGHTING. Draw attention to a specific item, such as artwork. Place an accent light at a 30-degree angle and focus its beam on the object. You need about three times the room's normal light to spotlight a focal point.

WALL WASHING works well when a wall or multiple objects on it are the focal point. To evenly light the area, place a row of accent lights on the ceiling 2 to 3 feet from the wall. Place them 3 to 4 feet from the wall if the ceiling is especially high.

CAN LIGHTS placed behind furniture and under plants shine up from the floor to create shadow drama on the wall. Affordable and flexible, these portable little lamps plug into wall sockets.

Draw attention to a piece of art with a tiny picture light you attach inside a bookcase niche. You will need to drill a hole through the storage unit that is large enough to pass the electrical cord through the back of the unit and to the socket below.

see the light

Mass square wall fixtures to get the impact of art while providing ambient light. This group of lights hangs on a board that hides the cords and drops them behind the wall. Bulbs change from the front, and each light turns on separately, which means you can create a light pattern (some off, some on).

103

subtle touches

tell your story

The quickest way to put your stamp on any space is to surround yourself with the family photos you love. Make a moving picture show by propping photos and mementos on a table or on picture shelves for a 3-D display. Arrange them in snap-together frames so you can change them like exhibits in a gallery.

find a focus

Whether you have built-in niches or stand-alone shelves to fill, gather similar items instead of a mishmash of things. For example, parade a cool, calm collection of pottery and resist the urge to mix in other categories of things. Play with a variety of shapes and sizes until your eye seems to dance easily along the display in a natural sequence; then you will know you have decorating rhythm.

let yourself glow

Pay attention to the decorating details of shops and restaurants so you can adopt them. This half-coconut shell votive candle, for example, was spotted in the powder room of a Cuban-style dining emporium. You may not have a cigar box, but you can substitute a wooden jewelry box, then cut open a coconut, fill it with white sugar, and settle a pretty votive into it.

please your senses

When you decorate a side table, toy with texture opposites—such as smooth, polished silver (shiny things attract attention) and wild, woodsy twigs or acorns. Stack CDs for sound effects to match your mood of the moment, and for freshness—don't count on ancient potpourris—bring in garden flowers or healthy, green plants.

105

106

where you bathe

The smallest room in the house—the bathroom—may be your biggest decorating challenge. It also can be the most fun.

The bathroom comes furnished with permanent fixtures that direct the style of the space. Unless your home is new, you inherit previous owners' style choices. The challenge is to adapt what's there to your own style. If you don't like the fixtures, no amount of accessorizing will hide them so you may decide to remodel. Plain, white fixtures are the best investment because of their versatility. You easily can accessorize basic white fixtures in a variety of ways. They also make the house more attractive to potential buyers when you decide to sell.

Conversely, you may have inherited a workable set of fixtures, are satisfied that everything in your bathroom is functioning well, and want to create your own private retreat. This chapter has practical and pampering ideas for your bathroom.

splish, splash

If wishes could be granted, you might ask for a luxurious place to linger and indulge your senses. Or you might request a room as efficient as a car wash with rinse and wax cycles. The bathroom, *opposite,* belongs to the first fantasy: Romantic white shower curtains surround an old-fashioned tub. Pale yellow walls create open, relaxing spaces, and shutters, impervious to water damage, let in the light while protecting privacy. Details matter: White towels imply clean-and-fresh simplicity, and a lovely, old curved bench doubles as a towel caddy. The decorative letters on the windowsill spell "envy." Do you?

wash & dry
in style

what you need

sanitary fixtures
basic tub/shower, toilet, and sink, preferably in white

vanity mirror

towel bar or stand

basic towels

lighting
overhead, vanity

small storage cabinet
medicine chest, wall-hung units with doors

closet or large storage cabinet
freestanding or built-in

shower curtain, liner

terry-cloth bath mats

window covering
frosted glass, simple blind

toilet paper holder

liquid soap container

toothbrush storage

plastic drinking glasses

laundry container
hamper, basket

what you'll want

new, updated sanitary fixtures
pedestal sink; tub/shower; toilet

spa chair
folding, upholstered, or rattan

focal-point storage
freestanding or built-in

updated lighting fixtures

new faucets/showerhead

power shower or shower massager

magnifying mirror
lighted, steam-resistant, extendable

large mirror
pier, full-length wall-hung, or freestanding

spa accessories
bath tray, candles, bath oils, relaxation CDs,
massage aids

window coverings
shutters, blinds

heated towel bar

decorative storage jars

shower soap & lotion dispenser

guest towels

do-it-yourself tub surround

Here's an inexpensive option for replacing the outdated tile in a bath surround: Remove the tiles and cover the walls with T-111 board, an exterior plywood with a slightly rough, grooved surface that mimics the look of barn siding. Paint the paneling with several coats of gloss white paint so the surface can be wiped down for easy cleaning.

list your
needs

Consider how you will use your bathroom. To share it with other family members, designate separate and shared zones. If guests also will use the bath, plan for storage that keeps the room neat and presentable.

good, clean fun

Give yourself and your bathroom a clean slate. After all, bathrooms are all about cleanliness, and you will feel more comfortable in your new home if you make cleaning, scrubbing, and organizing the bathroom top priority.

ERASE the signs of former owners. Remove switchplates, window treatments, socket covers, and small fixtures that don't match your style.

STRIP walls and floors of grime. Remove old carpeting and replace it with throw rugs until you can decide how you will treat the floor. Take down wallcoverings to prepare walls for painting.

CLEAR OUT linens, lotions, tools, and medications you no longer use. Store bathroom necessities only after you have cleaned storage spaces and painted the shelves or lined them with paper.

start anew

Go with white, at least temporarily. It's a color that signifies cleanliness and simplicity. You can add color after you have lived in the house for a while.

PAINT WHITE eggshell paint on your bathroom walls and woodwork. It's the easiest and least expensive material to use and provides a practical wipe-down finish. The soft sheen of eggshell looks better on woodwork than hard, shiny gloss and is less likely to attract beads of condensation from a shower.

HANG WHITE self-adhesive plastic pleated panels (available at home improvement stores) on your bathroom windows. This temporary window treatment makes a room feel new, clean, and private. The panels come with clips to raise them for maximum light.

SWITCH TO WHITE plates on light switches and electric sockets. Choose them to match the paint color.

BUY WHITE towels and a clear or white shower curtain to symbolize new beginnings.

APPLY WHITE to tiles. Did the bathroom come with stained tiles or tiles in colors that you dislike? Cover

them with several coats of white epoxy paint if installing new tile is out of the question. If the only drawback about the tilework is the dirty grout, whiten it with paint or bleach you'll find at home improvement stores.

beauty and the bath

Once the bath is comfortably clean, think of decorative and practical changes you would like to make. Do you need new fixtures, flooring, or tile? (See page 123 for buying information.) Do you want more storage, a shaving mirror, new lighting fixtures? Decide what you will keep and plan to work it into your scheme. For example, the ceramic tile color may not be your choice, but you decide to keep it because removing it will be a waste of material and time if it's in good condition. If the appliances are white but old-fashioned, you can update them with sleek, contemporary faucets.

hanging rods

Unless they are already installed by professionals, you may need to hang your own bathroom towel bars and shower curtain rods. Use these guidelines.

• **TOWEL BARS**

Allow at least 36 inches of towel-bar space for each person using the bath. Hand towels fit on 18-inch bars; bath towels need at least 24 inches. Set towel bars 58 to 60 inches from the floor.

• **SHOWER CURTAIN RODS**

Shower curtain rods come in straight bar, L-shape, and ring or oval shapes. Tub styles determine which shape is installed. Round and oval rods are suspended from the ceiling; L-shape rods have wall and ceiling support. Most rods are adjustable. Fit them directly over the tub, making the shower space as large as possible to help keep the shower curtain liner at a distance while you shower.

go hotel style

The payback for organizing and decorating the bathroom is the chance to supply it with the comforts of a private bath in a luxury hotel.

ARRANGE new white towels in a shiny, chrome hotel-style rack that hangs on the wall.

HANG over-the-door hooks on the door or fasten wall hooks on the wall to hold white terry-cloth robes.

LAY a bathtub valet across the tub and furnish it with candles, soap, and a sponge. Add matches too.

PLACE a bench near the tub. Use it to sit on or to hold bathside necessities.

BUY a shower soundtrack or soothing bath CD.

style on a budget

Update your towels with new display techniques. Fold bath towels lengthwise then roll them. Cluster the rolled towels in baskets or in wire crates. Or arrange them in a three-tiered basket stand.

wall stashes

Small bath spaces call for big ideas. Replace your bulky medicine chest with wall-hung boxes that have hinged doors to hide less-than-attractive containers. If the old chest was built into the wall, cover the gap between the studs with a large mirror that will make the room seem larger and give you a better look at yourself.

make it work
for you

what's your style?

If your style is simple and basic, pick up decorating cues from this clean white box of a bathroom. The room is pulled together with natural elements, and its bamboo-trimmed, cotton-backed matchstick blind offers light and privacy. Extra bath necessities are stored in a rolling cabinet, baskets, and boxes.

tickle your senses

water play

Not everyone thinks an efficient shower is the ultimate bathroom luxury. For some, it's a laid-back soak in the tub, where the body revels in silky waters and warms itself in relaxed oblivion. Instead of buying a pricey tub valet to hold your bath comforts, pull a $10 TV tray tubside.

116

A bath is more than a place of pure efficiency, cleanliness, and perfect organization. It also is the place for free-spirited, close-to-the-skin comforts.

for your eyes only

Create a private cocoon of visual indulgences:

COLOR. Balance that oh-so-clean feeling you get from smooth white tile and bright porcelain with a touch of color that gives your bath a mood that matches the way you want to feel. See the color tips below. If you can't decide on a single color, inject the room with a few colorful accessories, choosing no more than three colors and using pattern sparingly. Simple stripes work well. If bright colors aren't your style, go with neutrals in wood, marble, or ceramic tile.

LIGHT. Bathrooms demand intimate lighting to set a tranquil mood, so bright, overhead lights are a no-no. Try a low-voltage dimmer system. Or go low-tech with tubside candlelight. Drape a string of miniature white lights around a window or replace a ceiling light with a chandelier (have a lighting store electrify an old candle chandelier). Keep all electrical lighting well away from the tub.

color play

WHITE, the color of cleanliness and purity, looks clinical when not balanced by another color.

VIOLET, the color of dream and spirit, makes a room appear larger; it also promotes contemplation.

RED, the color of passion and action, makes a room feel smaller and cozy, and fills it with emotional energy.

BLUE, the color of calm, aids relaxation, honest communication, and sleep.

GREEN, the color of health and vigor, balances moods if it's not too dark or light.

YELLOW, the color of intellect and thought, promotes sunny feelings and a sense of well-being.

ORANGE, the color of conversation and sociability, elevates sensuality and strong feelings.

skin-sations

Appeal to your sense of touch with smooth, rough, soft, silky, wet, dry, warm, and cool textures.

TOWELS AND MATS. Buy thirsty towels, a cushy spa pillow for the tub, and a deep mat to sink your toes in. Install a heated towel bar.

SKIN SOOTHERS. While the tub is filling, add oils to the water. For an invigorating soak, rather than a relaxing one, use lemon juice and sea salts. Add a nature element to the tub surround—smooth, tactile stones that conjure up soothing images of the beach.

MASSAGE. A portable foot massager promotes blood circulation. Pat your "piggies" dry and rub on a cool foot gel to reinvigorate your feet.

water music

Get carried away with Bach for the bath or Handel's "Water Music." Bliss out on uplifting soundtracks.

aromatherapy

Improve your mood with gentle aromatics.

SCENTED CANDLES, SALTS, OILS & LOTIONS. Bath products made with synthetic oils lift your spirits simply because of the way they smell.

ESSENTIAL OILS. Pure oils extracted from plants have figured into cleansing rituals since early China and Egypt and are believed by some to have healing powers. Burn essential oils in a diffuser or buy candles that contain them. Lavender and bergamot are good choices for inducing relaxation. You will find small vials of essential oils in department store perfume sections or in herbal sections of health food stores.

good taste

Add drinks and treats to your bath regimen.

JUICE. Wine is one obviously relaxing bath drink. Experiment with orange or apple juice, or nonalcoholic champagne to tease your taste buds. Or indulge in a pretty orange mimosa made with equal parts of orange juice and champagne.

TEA. Choose green or black, hot or iced.

STRAWBERRIES & CHOCOLATE. Nothing matches the sweetness of this combination.

Combine the elements of natural and artificial light with mirrors to get the illumination and reflection you need for getting ready to go out and for relaxing when you return.

natural light

Natural light is optimal light. To achieve good natural light control during the day, hang a flexible window treatment that provides privacy but lets in maximum daylight. The best investment is a set of plantation shutters or high-quality blinds.

Or buy discount store inside-mount miniblinds to hang inside the window frame. A blind with standard white plastic or metal blades is always a good choice, while shiny, chrome blades express a sleek, chic style. Both are waterproof and easily cleaned with a dust cloth or a brush designed for blind blades. Another option is to install a classic white roller shade; it disappears behind a valance when rolled up to let in the light.

not-so-natural lighting

When the sun goes down, adequate lighting means a combination of electrical fixtures. Warm, white incandescent bulbs provide true and flattering light for grooming.

OVERHEAD. Depending on the size and shape of the room, one or more overhead fixtures provide the main or general light. Combination vents and lights often are installed in the ceiling above the toilet or near the shower. Shower, bathtub, and toilet alcoves require their own overhead light sources.

TASK. Additional light around mirrors focuses on the tasks of shaving or applying makeup. One idea is to flank the vanity mirror with identical sidelights; place the lights about 60 inches from the floor and 28 to 36 inches apart. For mirrors wider than 36 inches, choose an overhead strip with three to five lights. Place the strip at least 78 inches from the floor.

AMBIENT. At times, you will want soft, moody lighting to gently guide guests into the room or to barely light the space during a relaxing bath.

Dimmers. Sculpt bathroom space and create inviting ambience by replacing the wall switch with a dimmer switch. Or simply set a table lamp on a freestanding storage unit or shelf, plug it into a dimmer, and plug the dimmer cord into the wall socket. Dimmers save electricity and extend bulb life.

Candles. While bathing, you can burn votives contained in glass vessels. Be sure the containers are taller than the candlewicks. For safety's sake, never leave a burning candle unattended.

Novelty. Hang a lighted door drape, a string of party lights, or a strand of white miniature Christmas tree lights (get the white-wire version) around a wall-hung shelf or towel rack to add a temporary, fun light. Another idea: Attach a row of battery-operated tap lights on a wall for a fun and funky look. Press the tap lights into "on" positions for short periods of time.

the fairest mirrors

A basic bathroom requires a plain mirror over the sink, but you may find reasons to add more.

VANITY. A quality mirror tops the bathroom list of things you need for preparing to leave home for the day or a night out. For maximum clarity and style, avoid frosted-glass mirrors or mirrors etched with motifs. Instead, invest in plain, round, oval, or rectangular mirrors that will blend with any style of fixtures.

FULL-LENGTH. If you dress in your bathroom, fasten a full-length mirror to the front of a linen closet door, back of the bathroom door, or wall. For a more stylish version, buy a floor-standing mirror that pivots (you need a spacious bathroom for this). Another option: Buy a large pier mirror, set it on the floor, and lean it casually against the wall. If you need the floor space or want a more formal look, hang it on the wall.

MAGNIFYING. For shaving or applying makeup, attach a magnifying mirror with an extendable arm to the bathroom wall near an electric socket. Or choose a countertop makeup mirror that has lighting built inside.

NOVELTY. Hang a collection of small hand mirrors on a wall adjacent to a window. They will catch natural light and bounce it around the room. A similar idea: Insert mirrors into small picture frames and hang them in a grouping over a towel rack.

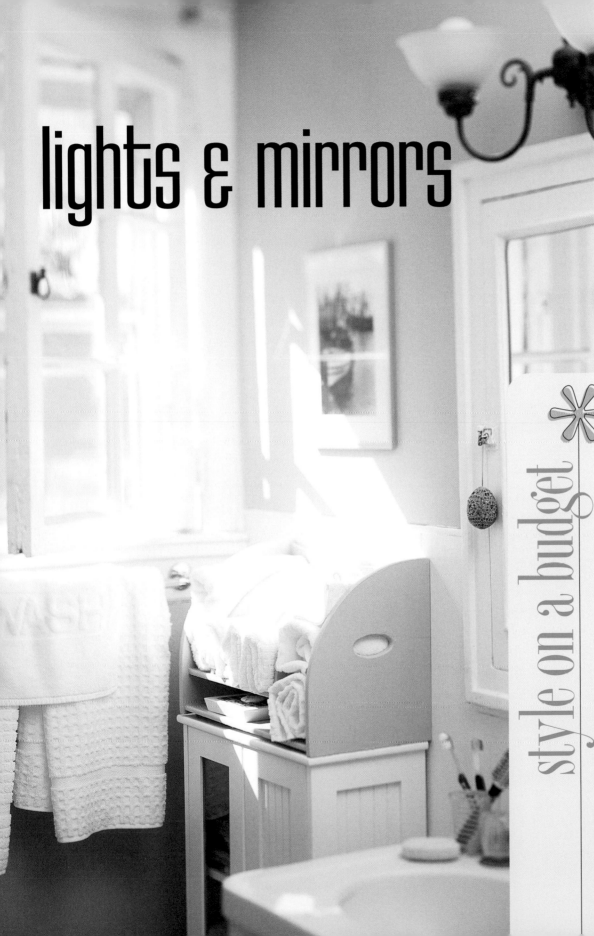

lights & mirrors

Nothing beats a bathroom with a generous source of natural light. Position a mirror on a wall adjacent to a window to reflect and bounce the light around the room. If privacy is a concern, treat your panes to the sheerest shades and curtains. Natural light will give you the truest reflection of yourself.

style on a budget

Bare is beautiful as well as inexpensive. If you have no privacy concerns for your windows, leave them unadorned. Natural light is a luxury any first home budget can afford.

freestanding closet

The most desirable storage is a built-in closet inside or adjacent to the bathroom. Not an option? Fit a freestanding unit inside the room for large necessities that don't fit in the medicine chest or in the cabinet under the vanity sink.

saving private spaces

stylish storage

A clean, well-organized bathroom creates a peaceful environment.

ADD SHELVES with brackets over the tub. If storage needs are great, add a second shelf over the door. Build shallow shelves between wall studs. When the medicine cabinet overflows, install a clear acrylic shelf on brackets above the sink.

FIND FREESTANDING STORAGE, such as a small cupboard, chest, or corner étagerè (French for standing shelves). If wall space allows, include a hanging cupboard or other decorative shelving unit.

HANG HOOKS for towels and robes. Sew fabric loops on towels for easier hanging. Remember to hang a hook on the back of the door too. Metal hooks, in a variety of styles and finishes, give a sleek, updated look. A door-hinge towel rack also works well and doubles as a robe or clothing hook. Clear the countertops by using wall-mounted hooks for blow-dryers or curling irons with long cords.

INSTALL ROLL-OUT DRAWERS. Similar to those used in kitchen cabinetry, they provide deep storage. Mount racks on the inside of cabinet doors or on shelves inside a cabinet. You can find roll-out drawers in kitchen and bath sections of home improvement stores.

REMOVE DOORS on a cabinet; replace the lower shelf with a laundry bin.

DECLUTTER by boxing up essentials that line a counter. A hair dryer can fit nicely in a decorative storage box. Use small boxes in complementary patterns and colors for easy-to-lose items such as earrings and pins. Turn bathroom essentials, such as cotton balls and swabs, into decorative accessories by storing them in metal-lidded clear plastic canisters arranged on a tray.

USE A BOWL, such as a dough bowl, wood bowl, or pottery piece, to hold towels for guests in a powder room. For guest soaps, try a vintage dish or plate rack filled with decorative plates.

shelf help

When you can't go outward to gain storage space, go up. Hang a tall, vertical shelf unit or rack on a wall (shop for a bookcase unit or a DIY rack) for bathroom towels and soap supplies. Shelve baskets to gather small items. Add a three-tiered rolling cart to move about.

plan
future changes

glass-block window update

1950s houses often come with wood-framed windows in tub/shower areas. Water ruins the window frame unless it is covered with a shower curtain. Replace the window with a vented glass-block window. Schedule the window replacement at the same time you replace the wall tile.

style on a budget

For a sophisticated, elegant, and clean look that's easy on the budget, buy clear or white bath accessories. Purchase just one paint color to brush on an accent chair, walls, and/or ceiling.

Bathroom fixtures and surfaces aren't the most exciting items to buy, but it's easy once you know the basics.

floors & walls

Choose floor and wallcovering materials that appeal to your senses and fill the needs of the space.

CERAMIC floor and wall tile is waterproof, stain-resistant and easy to maintain. However, its cold, hard surfaces amplify noise, offer no resilience or comfort while you stand on them, and can be slippery when wet. Glazed tiles, fired at high temperatures, are fairly impervious to stains, but unglazed tiles stain more easily.

LAMINATE tongue-and-groove looks-like-wood material is made from plastic. It's mess-free to install and exceptionally easy to maintain. Although it's durable, washable, and highly stain-resistant, it isn't waterproof.

RESILIENT or vinyl floors are comfortable to stand on, and glass containers are less likely to break when they fall on them. Relatively inexpensive compared to other products, vinyl sheeting and tiles are easy to maintain and available in thousands of designs. Vinyl tile floors have seams between each tile that may collect dirt over time. Inexpensive, self-adhesive tiles may shrink and pull away from each other, leaving gaps.

sinks

Vanity, wall-hung, and pedestal sinks are affordable. Reproductions of antiques and designer styles are available from bathroom fixture designers and contractors. Look for a model with few crevices and seams that will attract soap scum and dirt. All-in-one sink and countertop units that are undermounted (positioned just below the vanity top) are the easiest to keep clean.

VANITIES offer counter space for grooming tools, soap, water glasses, toothbrush holders, and regularly used bathroom items. They also provide undersink storage. Determine whether the base of the unit has been treated to withstand moisture.

PEDESTAL SINKS take up less space than vanities and make a small bathroom appear larger. Although they lack the storage space of a vanity, the open space beneath the sink can accommodate a wastebasket or a bathroom scale. Baskets of towels, bandboxes to hold extra tissue paper, and other creative storage solutions can fit under them. When purchasing a pedestal sink, consider which items you want it to hold: soap, water glass, cosmetics, or grooming aids.

WALL-MOUNTED SINKS take up less space than vanities but more than pedestal sinks.

FAUCETS AND HANDLES are sold by style, material, and quality. Choose high quality; cheap ones are not worth the hassle. Measure your sink for fit before buying.

tubs, showers & toilets

Look for these qualities:

TUBS commonly are manufactured in porcelain-coated cast iron, enameled steel, and fiberglass. Cast iron holds heat for long baths, has a lustrous finish, and often feels more substantial than other tubs. It requires sufficient support below. It also requires that the surrounding walls be covered with a waterproof material, such as a tile or a fiberglass shower enclosure. Enameled steel is similar to cast iron but is not as durable and doesn't hold heat.

SHOWER surrounds frequently are made from acrylics and fiberglass because they're lightweight, inexpensive, and easy to install and clean. Showerheads massage, pulse, are used as handheld units, and are adjustable for different heights. Water-efficient showerheads reduce water use. Oversize showerheads often measure up to 5 inches in diameter and offer a gentle cascade of water over a large area. Many extend on a long arm and adjust at several pivot points.

TOILETS are available in standard two-piece styles, sleek one-piece models, and designer shapes. One-piece units are easy to clean because there are no crevices between the tank and toilet. Some two-piece toilets have a "sanitary dam" that bridges this spot to prevent bacteria buildup. Two-piece units are available in several styles. Federal law prohibits the manufacture of toilets that use more than 1.6 gallons of water per flush. Unfortunately, some of these models don't flush as completely as older toilets. Toilets that operate by gravity alone many need two flushes, especially in areas with naturally low water pressure. Toilets with pressure-assisted flushing mechanisms are more effective; however, they may make more noise and are almost twice the cost of gravity models.

123

124

where you sleep

when you're all about experimenting

Your first bedroom is the perfect place to try your decorating hand and get a sense of your personal style. For example, this neo-bedouin look isn't for plain-vanilla types. But if savory hummus and kabobs whet your appetite and the feel of hot pavement under your feet makes you long for desert sands, why not give it a whirl? The most economical way to rock the Casbah is to paint your walls. Likewise, curtains made from single widths of sheer orange fabric can mimic the color of a flaming sunset. Choose a versatile bed frame so you can switch gears next year when you decide you're all about French moderne.

have it
your way

In story books, the bed is a safe harbor and place of ease. Are your bed and bedroom just the right size? Always look for the perfect fit to match your lifestyle.

In contrast to the function-junction ways of the cooking, eating, work, and bathing areas of your home, measure your bedroom by a different set of values. At its best, your bedroom gives you complete privacy and tranquility, while expressing your most personal tastes.

After you move into your first home, you may not have the luxury of pulling together your bedroom in the most natural order or sequence of decorating steps. Ideally, you would paint or paper the walls, carpet the floor, and hang perfect window treatments before you bring in the furniture, make your bed, and arrange your accessories (you would have time to add a bit of indulgence too). If you begin decorating when the moving van pulls up, just bring in the bed, make it up for the night, and climb in. You'll get to the rest later.

Wherever you begin, you will find bedroom-creating information and inspiration in this chapter.

discreetly feminine & flirty

Combine expensive with affordable, elegant with eclectic.
Balance a curvy, antique sleigh bed (quite pricey) with a dark
fireplace. Spiff up a secondhand wicker chair and wooden box
with coats of white paint; prowl estate sales for scallop-edge
bedding and an oval mirror.

inherently french

Instant French style happens when you dramatize a bed's featureless headboard with
a theatrical black and white toile backdrop. You can sew the backdrop from lightweight
fabric. If you don't sew, buy two curtain panels in a great accent fabric. Attach curtain
rod brackets to the wall behind your headboard, slip the tab-top curtains onto the rod
and into the brackets, and—voilà—you've checked into le Hotel des Sweet Oblivion.
Hang an Eiffel Tower souvenir plate and a couple of your initials (buy old printing or
signage letters) on wall-hung plate holders between the curtain panels.

what's your sleep style?

thoroughly modern & minimal

For an ethereally groovy vibe that's lean and clean, every detail counts. Here's where you can cut corners: Buy three solid-core birch plywood doors from a home improvement center. Measure to make sure that a foot of wood shows on both sides and at the foot of the bed when the doors are laid on the floor side by side with a mattress on top. Then splurge on a high-quality foam mattress—it doesn't require a box spring. (Using a spring mattress without a box spring cuts the mattress life in half.) Use a painting as a headboard and toss on a fake fur throw.

129

explore
your options

seek serenity

Give an upholstered headboard the soft touch with a linen slipcover. Hang a sari-print canopy to inspire exotic dreams—it's irresistible for "accidental" naps. To make the canopy, slip yardage on a ceiling-hung hoop (the kind used to hang mosquito netting) or drape fabric over a large, wall-hung bracket.

130

adopt a hand-me-down

go theatrical

Here are a couple of tricks to dress a bedroom for drama:

When you can't find the right accessories, start stitching. Splurge on a couple yards of 90-inch-wide velvet damask and hem it to make an elegant bedcover. Then "frame" it, like a work of art, with a "mat" of crisp white bed linens, folded down at each end of the bed. Sew curtains from striped sheets to add structure to a room lacking furniture or architecture. Transform an ugly dresser into an elegant dressing table with a simple, tied-on drape of white cotton.

Shop for used furniture. When your purchases come home, decorate around them to make them part of your family. How to love an old bed frame with a few scars: Wrap the head- and footboards with pretty cover-ups you've stitched yourself (see page 176 for tips on fitting slipcovers). To dignify a pair of mismatched nightstands, buy twin lamps that make them equal partners. Set the bed at an angle and surround the headboard with shutters that are not only pretty but also protective and practical—they redirect the strong drafts of dry winter heat from wall vents.

what you need

basic bed setup
foam mattress/platform, mattress/box spring/metal frame, or futon

mattress pad

pillows

sheets
full, queen, or king

blankets
fleece, cotton, or wool

comforter
cotton or synthetic filler

bedcover
quilt, chenille, or woven cotton

closet
built-in; freestanding wardrobe rack on wheels

storage for folded clothes
chest of drawers, built-in or freestanding closet drawers and shelves

nightstand(s)
box, decorator table, small chest, or rolling cart

lighting
bedside lamps, overhead fixture, recessed light

clock/radio

basic window coverings

mirror
vanity, full-length, or makeup

what you'll want

headboard or bed frame
painted, installed on wall, or freestanding

mattress upgrade
purchase a new mattress every 5 to 10 years

garment storage upgrade
antique armoire; remodeled closets; built-in entertainment unit

upholstered armchair or chaise

storage containers
jewelry, hatboxes, shoe boxes, jewelry trays, tie rack

rug
inlaid carpet or area rug

window covering upgrade

designer lighting fixtures

top-of-the-line bed linens

floor cushions

round coffee table

end-of-bed bench

feather bed

euro-square pillows

duvet

duvet cover

Little more than a bed, lighting, and storage are needed for the comfortable cocoon most people want in a bedroom. However, if you expect more function in your sleeping space, plan for additional furniture.

assess your assets

No one says you have to sleep in the "master bedroom" just because that's what it says on the floor plan of your new home. After all, you have the run of the house and can use the rooms as you like. For example, if you prefer to work late into the night and sleep until noon, a small, quiet room on the north side of the house may meet your sleeping needs better than the master bedroom on the street side. Consider its proximity to the bathroom. Make adjustments—such as keeping a water carafe on the nightstand—to avoid trips in the night.

Size up your furniture and clothing. Do you own a bed? Is it too big to round the corner in the stairs that lead to the cozy dormered attic space you have your heart set on for your bedroom? You may need to order a bed with a split frame to realize your plan. Do you like the size of your bed or do you want a bigger one? Is your closet big enough to accommodate your clothing or do you need more furniture for storage? Would a television set housed in an armoire be a plus in the room or a noisy disadvantage? What about a chair or floor pillows for lounging in a corner where you can read without disturbing your partner who is asleep? Do you want to set up a home office in one corner but have no desk?

Imagine your furniture and possessions in the room you have selected. You need at least a 21-inch-wide path to walk around the bed. Allow a little more than 3 feet for doors to swing open and 2 feet for drawers to pull out.

What is the condition of the floor? If you moved into an older home and aren't sure what lurks beneath the fibers of the carpet, you may feel uncomfortable about walking on it. You may decide that relieving the room of its ancient carpet and replacing it with new, do-it-yourself hardwood flooring is best. Rug

runners on each side of the bed make soft, warm surfaces to step onto first thing in the morning.

bring on the ambience

What atmosphere, mood, and style do you want your bedroom to express? Is it a leather-wood-and-steel, overtly masculine look that feeds your soul? Or do you prefer a calm and casual, soft and romantic atmosphere that allows for rest and relaxation? When you share your bedroom with someone, go democratic. Is the room strong enough for a man but decorative enough for a woman? Find common ground, such as neutral wall colors or colors you both agree on. Compromise on a bed to suit both sleeping habits. Allow equal parts of your personal differences to come in with accessories.

color tips

- **BLUE,** known for its calming effect, is America's number one bedroom color choice. Periwinkle blue—a violet blue—takes a sleeping zone toward a meditative attitude.
- **GREEN,** another color known for its tranquilizing effect, suits sleepers who love the soothing colors and grounding effects of green grass and trees.
- **RED** is great for a cozy love nest if you lace the walls with a lot of white or cream-colored trims. Covering entire walls with emotionally energizing red may leave you sleepless.
- **YELLOW,** when it is pale and sunny, lifts your mood in the morning. However, choosing the right yellow for a bedroom requires careful consideration. Remember that a sunny yellow on a paint chip triples in brightness after you get it on the wall. Lemon yellows may have too much zing and zest for a bedroom.

134

the bed

You spend about one-third of your life sleeping—that's a practical enough reason for buying a good bed. Your bed also is a place of dreams and plans—where your most secret thoughts find a home. It is a sanctuary for pain and pleasure, a comfort in sickness and health. Make it your prime piece of furniture.

plan your sleeping space

✳

Make your new mattress last longer by buying the accompanying box spring. Box springs in good condition take the brunt of the wear and keep the mattress looking lofty longer.

about a bed

136

pillow fight

If you and your spouse are fighting over bedroom style (one of you is into porcelain kittens, the other's into free-weights), go for a bed with unisex appeal. Clean lines and a steel frame say modern, while a rattan frame, such as this one, fits into a warmer traditional or country look.

Before purchasing a bed, read these tips:

bed frames

The first decision to make when buying a bed is size. Headboards and footboards add 3 to 4 inches of length to each end. Bed coverings add about 3 inches to the sides. Standard bed sizes are:
• Twin: 38–39×75 inches
• Extra-long twin: 38–39×80 inches
• Double/Full: 54×75 inches
• Queen: 60×80 inches
• King: 76–78×80 inches
• California King: 72×84 inches

Draw your bedroom dimensions on graph paper and sketch in the furniture and various bed sizes to determine which one works best. Allow 30 inches of clear space on at least one side of the bed for movement and changing bed linens. As you shop for bed frames, look for adequate support slats for the spring and mattress and determine whether the slats fit tightly into the frame. For beds designed to be used without box springs, a solid base provides support and even wear.

springs & things

Every 5 to 10 years, you'll need to replace the mattress on your bed. Test-drive a mattress before making a final decision. If you will share the bed with someone, take him or her along. Wear comfortable clothing and easy-to-remove shoes. Stretch out on the bed for several minutes. If you can slip your hand underneath the small of your back, the bed is too firm. The right mattress supports you so that you can turn easily with your hips and shoulders gently cradled. If you sit in bed to read or work, sit in the position you are likely to use. Firm does not always mean better; it comes down to personal preference and body shape. A good mattress supports your spine and has a bit of give at the pressure points, where your body sinks deeper into the mattress.

CHECK LABELS and cutaway samples to see how the mattress is constructed. The most common type of mattress is innerspring, which is made of tempered spring coils covered with layers of padding and upholstery. Compare the number of coils and their construction, the number of padding layers and their materials, and special features. The higher the number of coils, the better the bed will wear. A guideline is 300 coils for a double, 375 for a queen, and 450–600 for a king, each side topped with several layers of upholstery, one or more layers of foam, and a quilted pillow top.

ADDED COMFORT? Most mattresses are about 9 inches thick; some manufacturers offer extra deep mattresses, which may or may not mean more comfort. Comparison shop before assuming that deeper is better and be aware that your choices in bedding may be limited—you will need contour or fitted sheets with deep enough corners to accommodate a deep mattress.

CHECK THE WARRANTY. Some manufacturers offer sleep guarantees or test periods. If after buying the mattress, you find it isn't the right one, swap it. Check on delivery costs: If there is a charge for each change, it can get costly. Don't base the useful life of your mattress on the warranty, which is protection against defects and faulty workmanship, not loss of comfort.

tight spaces

• **BIG BED UPSTAIRS**
Larger mattresses and box springs may not fit around tight corners, up stairways, or into elevators. If you have one of these situations, shop for split box springs or even a split-spring mattress. Queen- and king-size box springs often come in two pieces. Other sizes have hinges in the middle. Split-spring mattresses typically cost more but are more versatile.

• **SITTING AND SLEEPING IN ONE SPACE**
Futons double as sofas by day and beds by night. The futon, which is the mattress, typically is made of cotton batting or a foam core covered with muslin or mattress ticking. For comfort, buy a futon with a mattress that is at least 8 inches thick. Choose a futon that folds out smoothly.

arrange
the furniture

divide and conquer

This studs-and-plywood headboard wall provides an ample backrest for vegging out while it hides the couple's closets behind. (You can purchase premade 4-foot-wide wall stud units at a home center.) Attach them to the floor and ceiling with crown and base moldings.

the right place

Feng shui, the ancient Chinese art of putting things in their place, offers these commonsense tips for creating the right energy flow in your bedroom.

BED. You want to be able to see the door, so place the bed on an opposite wall. However, don't place it directly opposite the door, or you'll feel like you're in the traffic path. Use a solid headboard placed against a wall to feel stable. Avoid a wall that is shared with noisy neighbors; don't place the head of your bed near a drafty window. Don't sleep under a structural beam—you don't want to feel that you're in physical danger. Allow a 30-inch-wide corridor on at least one side of the bed. To maximize space, tuck the bed in a corner so one side is against the wall. You'll need casters on the bed to pull it out for bed making and cleaning underneath.

MIRROR. Hang a mirror anywhere but opposite your bed; your reflection could wake you out of a restful state.

DRESSER, CHEST, OR ARMOIRE. Keep in mind the surrounding space each piece requires for safe and comfortable use. Allow 37 inches for opening doors and drawers. Give 24 inches of clearance to a chair pulled in and out in front of a dresser. Balance the weights of the storage pieces in the room. For example, after the bed is placed, put the largest piece in the largest remaining space. Place smallest pieces last.

TV, COMPUTER & EXERCISE EQUIPMENT. Ban them from the bedroom. If you can't do that, hide them in an armoire or behind a screen so you can get your rest.

PLANTS. Soften the reflective qualities of windowpanes by placing green plants in front of them. The plants will love living in the light.

hang up your clothes

baby grows up

Did your parents buy you a matching bedroom

set after you grew out of your crib? If they

intended the set as furniture for your first home,

oblige them. Treat the pieces to new white paint

and hardware and put them back to work.

what you want now

A bedroom usually has at least a small closet, but it may not be enough for you. Ask yourself:

• Do you need storage space for clothing beyond the closet and conventional chest or dresser?
• Do you have space for additional storage pieces?
• Do you plan to store seasonal clothing and bedding in the bedroom?
• Do you plan to use the bedroom for a home office, study, library, computer room, or hobby room?
• Will you store papers and records in your bedroom?
• Would a good purge of your clothing cut back your need for more storage?

make the most of your closet

Space may be hiding in your closet. If you've moved into an older home, change outdated rods, pegs, and hooks to get more use out of the closet's volume. Measure the height, width, and depth of your closet and head to a home improvement center to gather information on closet organizers you can assemble yourself. Don't buy on the first trip.

Compare the store's closet organizing plans to the size and shape of your closet to determine what works best for you. Draw your own plans that include high and low tiers for hanging shorter clothing; arrange tall slots for dresses and robes. Consider large stand-on-the-floor drawers that supply deep storage. Then buy what you need and assemble the organizers after you give your closet a new coat of paint.

freestanding storage

Chests of drawers and armoires are worth saving for. If you want furniture now, look for secondhand dressers and storage pieces that won't break the bank and can be replaced later. Or go with plain, ordinary utility: Store folded clothes on open shelves and hang loose clothing on an adjustable rolling garment rack hidden behind a screen.

For a second closet, angle a freestanding clothes rack in a corner behind an attractive new or vintage screen. Or make your own screen by hinging bifold doors from a home center and painting them.

what's behind the green wall

Here's how it looks on the other side of the headboard wall in the bedroom on page 138. Two inexpensive wood-and-plastic wardrobes (one for each spouse) stand back to back in the center of the 40-inch-wide corridor. On one side, hatboxes store little-used items. Wall hooks offer access to scarves and purses. A light string illuminates both sides.

141

mod for style

Check it out. The '70s are back—and so are affordable cubic

storage pieces that stack up to freestanding chests. They're

sold as units for closet use, but these cubes and double-

cubes are handsome enough for your bedroom.

space exploration

beyond the chest and closet

Containers are your best friends when it comes to extra storage—just remember where you hid everything.

DIRTY LAUNDRY. Choose perforated clothes hampers that are too handsome to hide. They keep dirty clothes out of sight and organized for the laundry. Buy two—one for washable clothing and one for dry cleaning.

UNDER THE BED. Use the space under your bed for heavy-duty plastic or cardboard storage boxes (buy boxes with tight-fitting lids to keep out dust). This space works well for out-of-season items, such as sweaters or blankets. Use it for belongings you don't need every day but that require climate control, such as photographs, books, gift-wrapping supplies, and heirloom linens.

UNDER THE TABLE. Skirt a particleboard table and stack boxes in the space underneath. Some plywood table bases are made with a shelf for stacked boxes.

TRUNKS. When you need maximum storage for items such as bulky quilts, add a vintage, reproduction trunk or chest at the foot of the bed. Wicker blanket chests are an easy-to-move alternative.

OUT OF THE BOX. Add a padded or wood bench and use the space underneath to stash out-of-season items in wicker or leather suitcases. Find decorative storage cubes with lift-off lids. These work well for matching bedside tables or at the foot of the bed in place of a conventional blanket chest. Specialty home decorating stores and catalogs carry variations of this versatile storage piece. Some have padded tops that work for seating at dressing tables.

VINTAGE FURNITURE. Get storage and style from mismatched vintage furniture. Try a burnished metal dresser or a 1930s dressing table with drawers. Look for shapely wood units to paint.

WARDROBE. Hang fabric panels on wire line or a drapery rod suspended from the ceiling to add concealed storage in a room. Choose washable cotton fabrics that complement your decorating scheme.

READING ROOM. Purchase matching bookshelf units to turn your bedroom into a reading nook. Choose contemporary- or traditional-style unfinished and ready-to-assemble shelves to paint or stain for a look compatible with your decor.

ANTIQUE ALLEY. Add storage to a traditionally styled bedroom by furnishing it with antiques. Shaker boxes in graduated sizes or wicker or wooden boxes enhance the look while hiding necessities and clutter. Find an antique steamer trunk or wood trunk for blankets, pillows, out-of-season clothing, or extra reading material.

SPECIALIZED STORAGE. Be creative with specialized storage. Add wood, woven, or art-paper-clad decorative boxes to store papers, magazines, crafts projects, or mending supplies. Cover plain cardboard boxes and their removable tops with heavy gift paper, brown kraft paper, or colorful wallpaper scraps for affordable, attractive storage containers.

DRESSER OR CHEST TOP. Use the space on your dresser or the top of a chest. Stack matching decorative boxes in graduated sizes to keep items such as earrings, costume jewelry, socks, tights, hose, or scarves handy for the morning rush.

clutter cuts

• **DIVIDE AND CONQUER**
Don't break down—break *it* down. Meet the clutter challenge head-on. In the same way that you meet the prospect of decorating your home by dividing it into small increments, take on clutter. One small step at a time will conquer it.

• **DOWN WITH DITSY**
The place for ditsy little baskets is inside drawers and out of sight, where they can keep the smallest items in line. Too many little (even well-organized) containers in a room has the look of clutter.

• **TAKE FIVE MINUTES**
Set the timer and make a list of storage problems in your house. Just listing them gets you closer to resolving them.

• **AVOID OVERLOAD**
Toss out while taking in—every time you buy a new item, get rid of something old.

Are you living with window treatments left by previous owners? Eventually, you may want to replace them with curtains, blinds, or shades more suited to your style and light-control needs. If your home is new and you need immediate privacy, hang temporary paper-pleat shades from home improvement stores. Attach the shade tops to the window frames by their self-adhesive tapes.

shades, blades & panes

Do your window treatments block out enough light for daytime sleeping? Do they let in enough light during the day so you can find your way through the room? Keeping light out of the bedroom is as important as letting it in or controlling its levels. Heavy draperies are seldom appropriate for the scale and style of bedrooms, so use a combination of light draperies, shades, or blinds.

ROLLER SHADES vary in price and quality. Choose cover material that is at least 6 millimeters thick, or they are likely to tear when pulled down or released. Vinyl covering or fabric-and-vinyl laminated combinations are good choices. Fabric stores carry kits and materials for fusing decorator fabric onto roller shades to coordinate with fabrics in your bedroom. Extra-heavy, room-darkening shades muffle light and sound and are worth the investment if you sleep during the day. Fit the roller shades snugly, leaving little space between the shade edge and the inside of the window frame.

VENETIAN, PLANTATION & MINIBLINDS offer more options in light control than roller shades. Although they operate the same, venetian blind blades measure about 2 inches wide and miniblind blades generally are 1 inch wide. Wood and metal blinds generally block more light, but plastic is less expensive. Measure the depth of your window to determine which will fit. Raise blinds to let in the light and view; lower them partially or fully for privacy.

Light control. Lower the blades to control light. Blades turned upward direct light to the ceiling; blades turned downward direct it to the floor. Look for blinds with little space between the blades when closed.

Noise control. Blinds do not offer as much noise control as heavy fabric shades and provide privacy only when they are completely closed.

Privacy control. If blind blades don't fit tightly and are turned downward, upstairs neighbors may be able to see through them. The same goes for blades turned upward—downstairs neighbors may be able to peer in.

PLEATED & CELLULAR SHADES are made of fabrics with varying degrees of translucency. Both raise and lower similar to blinds without pivoting blades for light control. Pleated shades fold accordion-style. The honeycomb construction of cellular shades has an extra fabric panel that provides additional light and sound control. Check the fabric to determine how much privacy and light control it offers; some shades are quite sheer.

VALANCES & SWAGS soften the look of the room and control light when used with shades or blinds by filling in the gaps between the window treatment and the window frame.

roller shades

- **DRESS-UP KITS**
Create custom fabric-covered shades with a no-sew fusible shade kit purchased from a fabric store. Kits are sold in 42-inch widths and can be cut to fit most windows. Typically, 2½ yards of 45-inch-wide fabric are needed. Follow directions for fusing the fabric to the shade. For added weight, attach tabs and a wood rod to the bottom of the shade.
Another option: Paint directly on a roller shade with paint markers for a custom, graphic look.

- **ROLLER RESCUE**
Tighten a shade that has lost its spring by unrolling it almost all the way. Leave the pin end in place and lift out the flat end. Roll the shade by hand and put the flat end back in place to tighten the spring and help the shade snap back in place.

bamboo too

When shopping for inexpensive shades or blinds in import stores, watch for design-conscious products. These simple but stunning bamboo panels, edged in black cotton, make graphic lines at a window when mounted outside the frame. The design changes as the shades go up and down.

dress
your windows

145

between the sheets

Thread count—threads per square inch—indicates sheet quality. A high number means finer, more tightly woven sheets. Muslin sheets at 130 are prone to pilling. Cotton or blend percales with 180–200 threads promise good value. While thread count is important, the quality of the thread is important too. A 280-count sheet with poor thread quality may not be as comfortable as a 200-count sheet with good-quality thread. Lay your cheek against the material for an indication of quality and comfort. Top-quality sheets, such as pima or Egyptian cotton have extra-long, lustrous fibers. The best buy? Linen sheets that soften with age or silk and satin sheets that caress your skin.

make
your bed

bed making, american-style

A well-made bed is a little luxury you can give yourself every day. Here's how it's done in the States:

BED SKIRT. Hide the metal supports and rails with a bed skirt or dust ruffle.

QUILTED PAD. For maximum mattress protection, cover the mattress with a quilted pad that has fitted corners. Option: Top the pad with a feather bed for extra softness.

BOTTOM SHEET. Use percale sheets in cotton or a cotton blend to avoid shrinkage. With a fitted sheet, begin at a top corner and move around the bed to set the sheet in place (purchase a fitted sheet with extra-deep pockets if you have a feather bed on the mattress). If using an unfitted (flat) bottom sheet, center the sheet over the mattress pad. Tuck under at each bottom corner. Pleat and fold over and under to make hospital corners.

TOP SHEET. Align the sheet with the bottom sheet. Tuck under at the bottom of the mattress. Pleat the bottom corners, fold down, and tuck in for a neat finish. Smooth the sheet at the top of the bed. Option: Make the bed with the wrong side of the top sheet up; fold it over the top of a comforter to reveal the right side.

BLANKET, COVERLET, OR COVER. Top with a blanket, coverlet, or comforter, depending on the season. Use a blanket with a bedspread or quilt for extra warmth. For a neat look, line up the bottom of the comforter with the footboard rail. Lay an extra blanket at the end of the bed.

PILLOWS. Add 26-inch Euro-square pillows for reading, standard pillows for sleeping, and an accent pillow.

quick bed, euro-style

To eliminate the blanket, bedspread, and top sheet from your bed-making routine, choose a cotton or down duvet and a washable duvet cover (an envelope of sheetlike fabric that slips over the duvet like a pillowcase). The duvet cover is washable and replaces the top sheet and bedspread. Cover the mattress with a fitted sheet. To make the bed, toss the pillows in place, shake out the duvet to fluff it up, and lay it loosely over the bed. For seasonal comfort, buy two duvets—a lightweight one for summer, a heavier one for winter.

DUVET OR COMFORTER. The ideal duvet, a down- or feather-filled comforter with a woven fabric cover, measures at least 18 inches wider than the bed and provides lightweight, self-adjusting warmth.

Fill. When buying a duvet, note the fill power (number of cubic inches an ounce of down occupies). The higher the fill power (300 to 700), the more ability the comforter has to trap air and provide greater warmth. Also note the quality of the fill. The best natural filling is white goose or duck down. A "down and feathers" label indicates a lesser filling—feathers mixed with a larger amount of down. "Feathers and down" means more feathers, less down.

Construction. Thread count of the cover fabric determines how well the fill is contained. A higher thread count and tight stitching keep the duvet from leaking feathers or down. Choose between baffle covers—tightly walled squares that keep the fill high and balanced—or channel constructions that allow you to shift the duvet contents. While not as warm or natural, nonallergenic down alternatives are available. Synthetic, wool, and cotton downs weigh more but have the advantage of washability. Washable comforters, often sold in complete bed sets, do not have removable covers.

pillow talk

When deciding what to lay your head on for the night, determine your favorite sleeping position. Soft pillows are for stomach sleepers and usually are all down. A medium pillow, for back sleepers, will be half down and half feather. A firm pillow, for side sleepers, will be about 90 percent feather.

• **DOWN AND FEATHERS:** Down pillows can cost $25 to more than $200. As with comforters, price depends on the proportion of down to feathers in the filling. The more down, the more expensive the pillow.

• **ALTERNATIVES:** Better polyester pillows are filled with hollow-core fibers coated with silicone. Foam rubber wears out sooner and won't conform as easily to your head. For allergy sufferers, antibacterial cotton-filled pillows can offer some relief.

In your bedroom, you can justify a little splendor or va-va-voom. Look to textures, rather than colors and shapes, to set the tone. Here an exotic fake fur pillow and rug, a woven wicker lounge chair, and a hand-stitched quilt bring on the luxury notes.

bedside alternatives

Guest room nightstands don't require drawers and shelves because visitors aren't likely to store items in them. Use this bedside space for a vintage table or small storage chest that doesn't work elsewhere in your home. You can use it to store extra or little-used supplies.

ROLLING BOOK STACK. When favorite books add up at your bedside, stack them on a rolling plant dolly (you'll find one in a garden supply store). Use the top of the book stack as a shelf, where you can put your cell phone and pick up your remote to control the TV or soundtrack from your bed. This functions well if you have a wall-hung bedside lamp or a pendent lamp that hangs from a cord attached to a hook on the ceiling.

LEDGES OR BOXES. In a tight squeeze of a room, attach 4-inch-wide ledges and boxes from mail-order catalogs on the wall to hold books, candles, clocks, and phones.

SHOE STACKERS, available in closet organizing sections of home improvement or discount stores, work as bedside storage when you stack a small unit on a larger one. This gives you open-shelf storage that can move on to new uses after you save enough money for a nightstand upgrade.

DECORATOR TABLES. Try round, fabric-covered decorator tables, available in 20- or 24-inch diameters. You can find them in fabric stores, import stores, and discount stores. Buy the coordinating glass tops to protect the circles of decorative fabric you put on them.

nightstands

Nightstands are most convenient when they are just a few inches taller than the mattress—about 27 to 33 inches high. When buying a nightstand, evaluate how you'll use it and what you will store in it. Tissues, eyeglasses, and books are easier to reach in nightstands that have shelves rather than drawers.

For items you like to keep hidden, choose a nightstand with at least one drawer. Be sure the top is large enough to accommodate an alarm clock, a photograph, a decorative item, and perhaps a phone. If the room has no fixed lighting beside the bed, you also need space for a small table lamp. Choose a nightstand that complements the bed size and style (it does not have to match). Small chests work well beside twin beds but look out of place next to king-size beds. Two nightstands need not match but should be similar in size.

morning, sunshine

Can you reach for the alarm clock without upsetting that glass of water? Practice minimalism on top of your nightstand. Choose five items that are meaningful and tell your story—a travel photo hung on a lamp stem by a magnet, a favorite scent, a stylish lamp, and a couple of books.

bedside manners

style on a budget

No nightstand space on one side of the bed? Install a narrow shelf on wall brackets to hold a lamp, alarm clock, or other items. Be sure the shelf allows adequate space to access the bed.

lights out

After the sun sets, you'll need artificial lighting to help you identify the contents of your drawers and closets, find the remote, check your reflection in a mirror, or read in bed. Before you go to sleep, drop a little oil of bergamot on the lightbulb in your bedside lamp. The heat from the light will emit the scent, creating a relaxed mood.

Your bedroom needs flexible lighting that can change from functional to romantic to suit the need and mood of the moment.

night-lights & lamps

Choose lighting that works, technically and aesthetically. In a sleek, contemporary room, use lighting that creates a dramatic interplay of light and shadow. Preserve the genteel mood of a traditional room with soft lighting. Create a playful attitude in a hip-chic space with quirky, artful lights.

BEDSIDE LAMPS on each side of the bed make reading and working in bed convenient. Typically, nightstand lamps are shorter than traditional table lamps to allow for reclining while you read. Place the bottom of the shade at about cheek height so the glare of the bulb does not cause eyestrain. Flared lampshades help to direct light toward the bed and working or reading material. Arrange lamps so that you don't have to get out of bed to turn them off. Bedside lamp styles need not match exactly but should complement each other. Choose fixtures of roughly the same height or purchase matching shades to unify them.

SCONCES that cast light downward are alternatives to nightstand lamps and require no nightstand space. Up-cast sconces provide good mood lighting but provide poor reading light.

SWING-ARM LAMPS, mounted on the wall above the nightstand, are perfect when the bedside table is tiny or nonexistent. Consider one with three-way switches or dimmers if you like soft mood lighting.

PENDANTS hung close to the wall serve the same purpose as sconces or swing-arm lamps. The disadvantage of using sconces, pendants, or swing-arm lamps near the bed is that they dictate the placement of the bed and may be in an awkward position for rearranging furniture. If you use pendants, position them so that the shades are above your head and the light cascades over your shoulder.

TRACK OR RECESSED lighting can be used for reading light or as accent lighting. A row of lights over the head of the bed provides reading light; a span elsewhere may emphasize artwork or furniture.

VANITY LIGHTS, also known as dressing lights, offer flattering illumination when at face height. The height varies depending on whether the mirror is intended for seating or standing illumination. Provide balanced lighting on each side of the mirror.

which bulb

Soft-white bulbs provide the best light for bedrooms. Colored bulbs may make matching clothes or applying makeup difficult. Use 60-watt bulbs at the bedside. Consult the fixture label for recommended wattage and never use a higher-wattage lightbulb than the fixture manufacturer recommends.

When bedside lamps have two bulbs with separate pull switches, you can adjust the light level up or down. For more flexibility, choose bulbs of different wattages, perhaps 60 and 25. Turn on both for reading, only the brighter bulb for an intermediate level, or only the dimmer bulb for mood lighting.

design tips

• **LIGHTING A DARK ROOM**
A dark-colored room requires more light than a light-colored one. If you paint your bedroom a darker color, you may need to change your lamps, adding more translucent lampshades or brighter bulbs to make up the difference.

• **ON APPROVAL**
The color of every surface—walls, floor, ceiling, and furnishings—either reflects or absorbs light. The color and brightness of the light your eye sees is the combined product of the actual light plus its reflections. Because so much depends on the room itself, try out a new lamp, fitted with the right bulb, before buying.

152

a few good rules

room arranging

※ corridor living rooms

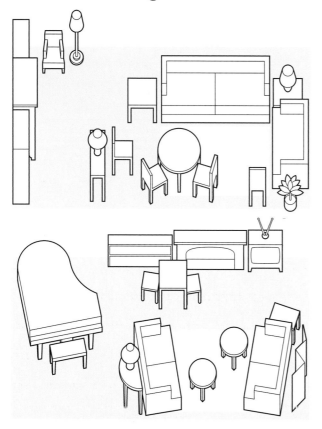

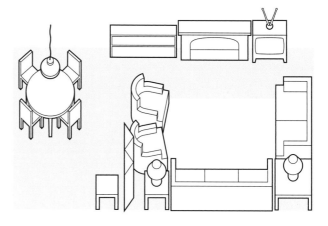

Corridor living rooms connect front entries to the rest of the house. Here the front entry is at the lower left corner; entry to the kitchen is straight across the space. Kitty-corner to the entry is a hall to the bedrooms. Arrange furniture in corridor rooms so traffic flows around—not through—the conversation area. Avoid placing seating pieces along walls because that encourages people to walk through the grouping; group seating pieces together to direct people beside or behind them.

getting a total look

A well-decorated home is one cohesive whole with rooms that blend and relate to each other like members of a family. To bring together the separate parts of your home, keep the following top 10 room arranging tips and decorating rules in mind.

1. DECORATE WITH PAIRS. "Mix, don't match" is the most often quoted decorating rule. Such good advice leads to informal, relaxed homes with a lot of personal style. However, in the hands of overenthusiastic followers, chaos or busyness may develop. For balance, blend in "decorate with pairs," a tried-and-true rule that always works to help build a solid foundation, hold a room together, and provide instant harmony. Matching pairs of lamps, chairs, or side tables bring home a bit of

✳ tunnel living rooms

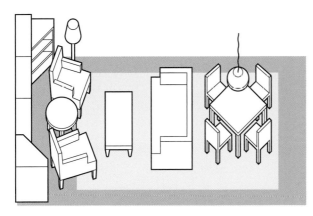

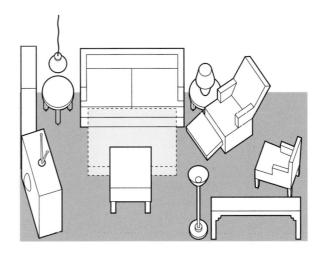

Living rooms or family rooms with single entrances are apt to appear long and narrow. Change the look to wide and spacious by breaking up the length of the room with furniture. Pieces placed at an angle, tables with curves, or couches set crosswise are options for broadening the look and feel of a room—and for getting one space to serve two purposes. These furniture arrangements also direct traffic gently around conversation areas rather than straight through them to the far wall.

symmetry and order that results in a feeling of safety, security, and unity. For example:

• **Side by side.** Hang two pieces of same-size wall art together for impact (make sure they have matching frames). Place two Euro-style pillows at the head of your bed to give it a visual lift. This will also provide more comfort while viewing television in bed. Pair up candlesticks and toss matching pillows on both ends of a sofa.

• **Two's company.** For intimate dining, face a couple upholstered chairs across a small, square table. Center a hanging light (in lieu of a centerpiece) over the table.

• **Two become one.** Turn a pair of mismatched windows into a single unit with a window treatment to provide a focal-point backdrop for informal furniture elements. Or unify two sofas of different lengths and styles with matching slipcovers.

• **Two's better than one.** A pair of lamps set side by side on an entry table makes a dramatic design statement. Two matching upholstered chairs are more striking than the usual table/vase/one-chair arrangement in an entryway. In the bathroom, dual pedestal sinks create a democratic feeling.

room arranging

❋ L-shape living/dining rooms

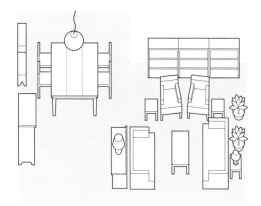

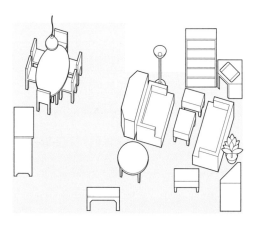

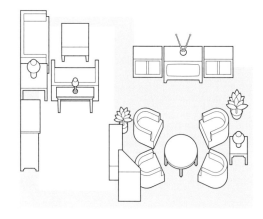

Some homes have an L-shape room—generally intended for living and dining. Typically, the short end is labeled "dining area"; the rest of the space is for living. While the open space is a plus, it can look busy if small-scale pieces fill the room or the traffic flow is clumsy. Of course, you needn't define the space according to the builder's floor plan. Decide where you'll dine and where you'll relax. Then choose and arrange furniture accordingly.

getting a total look

2. CREATE FOCAL POINTS. The goal of any room arrangement in your house is a simple grouping of furniture pieces that works toward its purpose—dining, sleeping, working, or relaxing. Achieve a focus for each room through a visual reference point—an architectural feature, such as a fireplace, or a dominant piece of furniture—around which all other pieces are oriented.

3. KEEP IT SIMPLE. The pared-down look is an elegant approach to first home decorating. The simple look has an unexpected benefit: Less furniture costs less money. Buy the best you can afford. This may mean buying one good-quality piece and making do with less expensive interim pieces until you can afford the furnishings you want.

4. DIRECT TRAFFIC. Pay attention to how people move through your house. Eliminate bottlenecks by moving aside furniture pieces that stand in the way. Create easy access through your rooms with 3-foot-wide passages that suggest where you want traffic to flow.

✻ multipurpose dining rooms

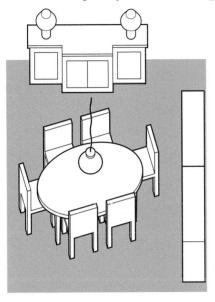 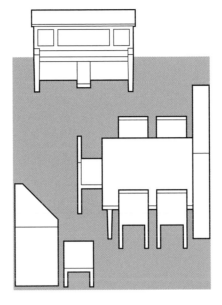 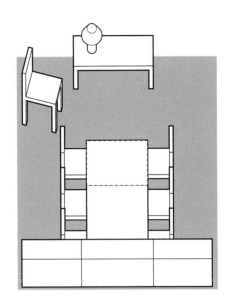

Work, hobbies, and many more first home activities often take place in the area designated for dining. Choose and arrange furnishings to accommodate several purposes. Typically, the dining room is between the kitchen and living room, so keep traffic flow in mind. Choose a table with a tough surface to handle a range of activities and choose chairs that do more than sit pretty. In every variation of these arrangements, adequate lighting is important, so add lamps in each task area.

5. ARRANGE ISLANDS OF COMFORT. Tighten furniture into islands to serve well-defined purposes. Use furniture to define areas within a room. For example, place a console table behind a sofa that sits at a right angle to a doorway. This creates a back "wall" for a conversation group in the living room. An area rug also defines an island of furniture. Or place a seating piece at the foot of the bed to extend the relaxing comfort in your bedroom.

6. WATCH SCALE. The British have a word for small rooms decked out in small-scale pieces or mini-patterns: twee. It's not a good thing. Avoid the dollhouse look by choosing one or two significant pieces for each room. These pieces, along with any strong architectural element such as wall paneling, give small rooms substance.

7. SET THE STYLE FOR YOUR HOME AT THE DOOR. Use entry furnishings consistent with the rest of your home. If you have no entrance inside the door, play up the front door on the outside. Add molding around the door frame and to the door. Paint or stain the door an inviting color that gives a hint about what lies inside. On your doorstep, add plantings in containers similar to those inside.

room arranging

✳ den/guest rooms

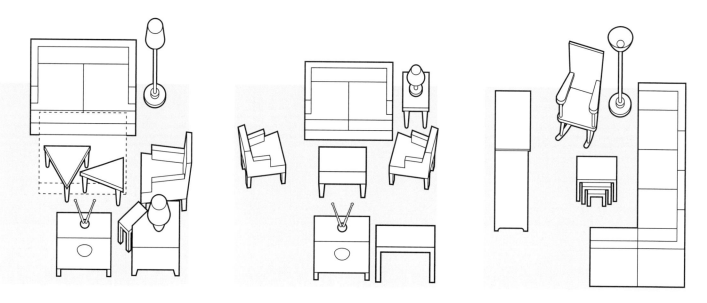

A spare bedroom is a space opportunity waiting to happen. Consider your second bedroom as a guest bedroom as well as a quiet den, TV room, or home office. Dual duty is doable, but the average spare bedroom can't accommodate much more activity than that. The key furniture choice in these arrangements is mobile occasional tables that make opening up the bed a breeze.

getting a total look

8. BE CONSISTENT. Use similarities in furniture style throughout your home, building a wardrobe of mix-and-match pieces that express your personality and lifestyle. Explore discount warehouses and mail-order outlets for good-quality furnishings at reasonable prices. Don't buy because the price is right; as the saying goes, "You get what you pay for." Make "browse first, buy later" your furniture shopping credo. It doesn't pay to be impulsive with high-ticket items. Peruse books and magazines to learn about style and construction; then compare items in all price ranges.

9. DEFINE YOUR HOME WITH PAINT. Apply the furniture consistency rule (number 8) to paint and wallcoverings. Use the same woodwork color throughout the house for a continuous, seamless style. When choosing your color palette for the house, choose wall colors with a similar lightness or darkness to avoid sharp contrasts or jarring changes from room to room.

✳ bedroom suites

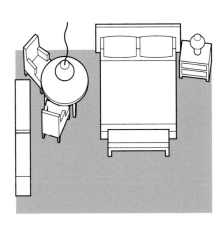  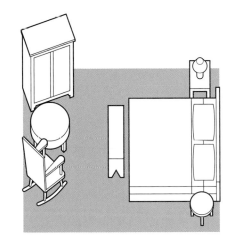

Turning a bedroom into a suite requires a little ingenuity. First free up floor space. Then look for pieces to create a relaxing grouping. Look at chairs and small tables not usually grouped with bedroom sets to expand the spacious feel of the room. For inspiration, remember the elements of favorite hotel rooms you used while on vacation. The goal is to create a room that includes an escape area as well as a sleeping platform. Choose bedcoverings and window treatments that bring out your vacation theme.

• **Draw lines around a room** with painted or stained woodwork. Boring, featureless woodwork is best painted the same color as the walls, but beautiful woodwork deserves to be a main attraction in a room. Emphasize it with high-gloss or semigloss paint that contrasts with the wall color. Or give it a different color—on light walls, give the woodwork a slightly darker color. Or reverse the effect with lighter woodwork on slightly darker walls.

• **Unify furnishings** with matching stains and paints. Coordinate upholstery fabric colors.

• **Accentuate ceilings.** Often ignored, ceilings are simply painted white to reflect the light coming in through the windows. If your home has plenty of light, extend your scheme with colored ceilings and lighting fixtures that complete the look.

10. LET YOUR DECORATING STYLE EVOLVE. Decorating a home is a lifelong process that changes as you change. It's an unfolding experience that lets you express yourself. Your patient, one-at-a-time purchases will pay off in a distinctive decorating style. Enjoy the time you spend doing it.

how you make it

GO DIGITAL. Immerse yourself in the singular perfection of a flower, leaf, or pod by making it larger than life. For about $9 a square foot, copy or print centers can enlarge a digital image to poster size.

1 Take the picture yourself with a digital camera set on high resolution. To get an image of a flower, leaf, or pod only—with no background—photograph it outdoors against an all-white backdrop, such as foam-core board. Hold the flower vertically and shoot away from the shadow. Download your image and e-mail it to the copy center or take the camera to the copy center and download the image there.

2 For the film camera method, photograph your flower, leaf, or pod image as described, *above.* When you take the film to the camera store for development, ask the film developer to supply a photo CD with the prints. Or a copy center can scan a print to create a digital file for about $10.

3 Ask the copy center to print your super-size image on flat, semigloss, or glossy poster paper. Tell the technician what size the poster should be and where to position the image.

4 Mount the poster on foam core and display it in a clip frame.

what you need:

flower, leaf, or pod

digital or film camera

computer (optional)

e-mail (optional)

9 × 12-inch foam-core board

CHEAP AND EASY. The expense of this project depends on the fabric you choose. The pop-art decorator fabric, *opposite*, runs about $48 a yard. For something more budget-friendly, check the bargain tables at a fabric store.

1 Using the instructions that came with it, assemble the canvas-stretcher frame. The finished size is 48 × 72 inches.

2 Iron the fabric then place it facedown on a clean, flat surface. Center the frame over the back side of the fabric. Ask a friend to help you stretch the fabric on the frame. One of you stretches the fabric over the edges of the frame and holds it in place while the other staples it to the back of the frame.

3 At the center of one long side, use one staple to fasten the fabric on the back side of the frame. Then go to the center of the opposite side; stretch the fabric gently and fasten with a staple. Repeat this procedure on the short sides.

4 Working outward from the center point on one long side, gently stretch the fabric and staple it every two or three inches until you reach the corners. Repeat on the opposite side. Staple one short side, then the opposite one. To secure the corners, fold the fabric neatly in hospital corners, *right*, and staple.

what you need:

2 yards of 54-inch-wide fabric

two 72-inch canvas stretchers

two 48-inch canvas stretchers

woodworker's hand stapler

staples

BE AN ARTIST. Artist's canvases provide an easy, versatile way to put bold colors on your walls. Ready-made canvases are already stretched, stapled to frames, and primed. Find them at art or hobby stores.

1 Choose a series of wall paint colors for your canvases. Three sources of inspiration:

SEASONS OF THE YEAR. The natural seasons of the year suggest a year-round color palette. Spring greens revitalize rooms in late winter. Blues cool them in midsummer. For fall-style warmth, choose reds and yellows. The colors for the canvas series in this dining room were inspired by blue and green shades of songbird eggs.

YOUR PERSONAL STYLE. Select a series of hues that signify your personal style. Are your signature colors cool and understated, warm and vivid, or bold and brilliant?

PAINT MANUFACTURER'S CARDS. Study paint manufacturer's color-combination cards exhibited with the full range of interior and exterior paints.

2 With a paintbrush intended for latex paint, paint one color on each artist's canvas. If needed, apply a second or third coat.

3 Hang the canvases, leaving 2-inch spaces between them. If you tire of your palette, paint over the colors with new ones.

what you need:

four 24 × 36-inch artist's canvases

one quart of latex interior house paint for each canvas

latex paintbrush

INTERIOR SEDUCTION. Add your own artful trim on a plain sheet or duvet cover. You can design your own stencil for a signature look or use a ready-made stencil purchased from a crafts or hobby store.

1 Prewash the new sheet or duvet cover; allow it to dry and press flat.

2 To make a stencil, cut your own motif from self-adhesive vinyl (the kind used for shelf liners) using a sharp utility knife. If you plan to use a ready-made plastic stencil, buy spray adhesive to adhere it to the fabric.

3 Lay out the fabric on a large, clean, flat surface; plan the arrangement of the overall design—a border around the piece, a single border along the top edge, or motifs scattered freely over the surface.

4 Using a small amount of fabric paint in a dish, dab the stencil brush or sponge onto the paint, pouncing it quickly up and down on the dish until the paint is thinly spread over the entire brush or sponge surface. Then pounce the brush or sponge over the open areas of the stencil; fill in the design with paint, being careful to keep excess paint from bleeding under the edges of the stencil. Repeat to complete the design. When dry, follow the paint manufacturer's heat-treating directions to preserve the design.

what you need:

sheets or duvet cover

self-adhesive vinyl and utility knife or purchased stencil and spray adhesive

fabric paint or acrylic paint mixed with a fabric-friendly conditioning medium (all available at crafts stores)

stencil brush or sponge

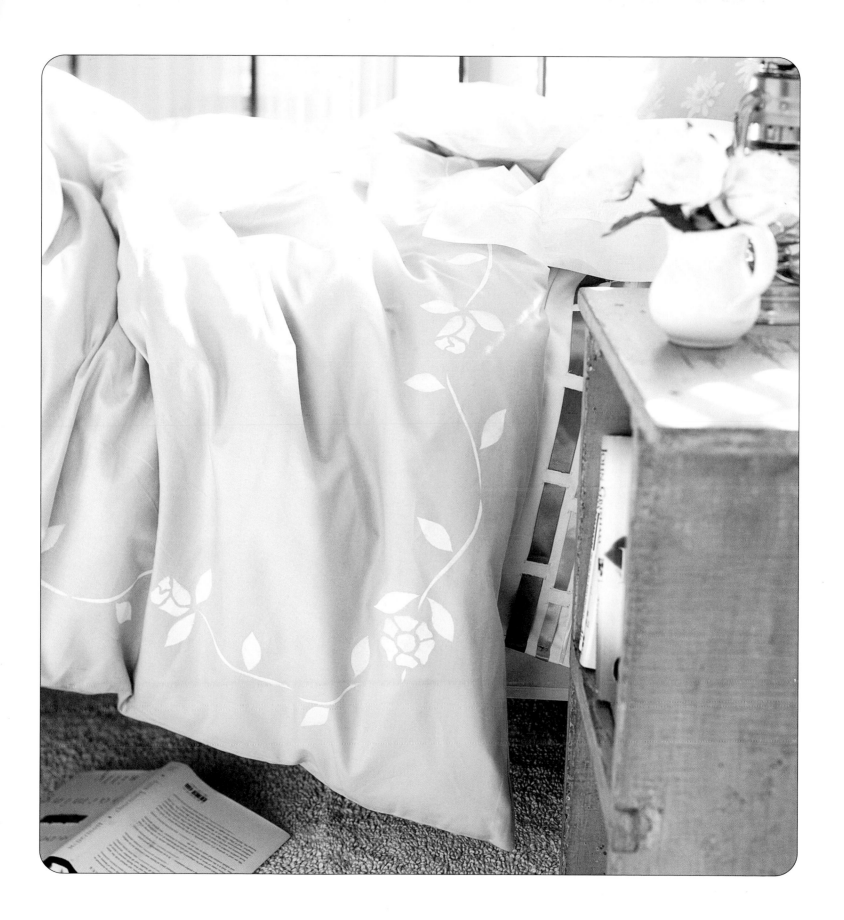

SEW SIMPLE. Slip a down duvet into a duvet cover—as you would a pillow into a pillowcase—for Euro-style bed making. The finished size for this cover is 86 inches square, the average size of a down duvet. Adjust the measurements if your duvet or comforter size is different.

1 Prewash the fabric. When dry, rip off the selvages (finished edges).

2 Tear most of the fabric instead of cutting it with a scissors. Working *with* the grain of the fabric, tear four 24 × 101-inch panels. Tear twelve 1 × 101-inch strips. With scissors, cut the narrow strips into 8-inch lengths for "ties."

3 With wrong sides facing and using ½-inch seam allowances, sew the four large panels together along the long edges. The seam allowances with their frayed edges will be on the outside (front side) of the duvet cover.

4 For the back of the duvet cover, tear a piece of muslin the same size as the front.

5 Pin the backing to the front of the cover, wrong sides facing. Fold up a 3-inch hem (border) on the sides and bottom, leaving frayed edges visible. Fold the two bottom corners into hospital corners; tuck excess fabric inside. Do the same to the back. With the smooth (wrong) sides facing, pin the top and bottom of the cover together, matching the edges. Stitch together along the frayed edges of the hem border. Finish the top edges of the cover with simple rolled hems.

6 The surface "ties" of the cover are decorative and don't really tie layers of fabric together as in quilts. Attach the 8-inch strips to the topside of the cover by hand. To do so, pinch the strip at its middle and hand-sew tightly to the cover. Sew them on the cover every 5 inches in rows that are 5 inches apart.

7 Attach pairs of strips along the open end of the duvet cover as ties to close the cover after you insert the duvet.

what you need:

5⅔ yards of 120-inch-wide bleached muslin sheeting (available in fabric stores)

sewing machine

white thread

draperies ✳

SHEER GENIUS.

It's like wearing a slip under a see-through dress. As with clothing, translucent sheers are becoming the window dressing of choice. If privacy is an issue, layer them over opaque curtains for a flirty couture style that will make you see your view in a different light.

scarf dance With two big clips from an office supply store (see detail, *left*), fashion a dramatic flourish at your window. First mount a 36-inch length of threaded rod from a hardware store as a curtain rod; buy threaded rod nuts and screw them onto the ends of the rods as finials. Slide a sheer "slip" panel onto the rod. Then, with the office clips, fasten the corners of one end of a dressy scarf onto the rod over the first panel, leaving a loose, stylish curve at the center.

sheer drama Two lengths of green organdy go powder soft when layered over a sheer, white panel. Hang a white ready-made sheer curtain on a tension rod inside the window frame. Then mount a wood curtain rod over the window frame. Hem the tops only of the two lengths of organdy (check the bridal section of your local fabric store). Hand-sew the tops of the organdy panels to the curtain rings at 8-inch intervals.

peekaboo lace Loop a length of lace over a curtain rod hung from the ceiling (place the rod about 4 inches out from the front of the window). You need twice the length of the height of the wall—$5\frac{1}{2}$ yards for an 8-foot-high wall. For privacy, hang a length of white organdy on a tension rod inside the window frame.

CONTEMPORARY SPIN. Punch up readymade curtains with an array of silvery grommets. Designed to mimic old-fashioned eyelet fabric, the metal Os create a modern look with no-sew ease. Grommets—also called eyelets—are found in crafts, hardware, and fabric stores.

1 Lay the curtains on a hard surface. Arrange the grommets in a pleasing random pattern (see the photograph, *below*). Cluster trios of small grommets and let larger ones float singly.

2 Mark the centers of the grommets on the curtains with a fabric-marking pen or pencil.

3 Following the manufacturer's directions, cut small holes on the marks and insert the grommets. Snap them together with the grommet tool in the package or one purchased separately.

4 Hang the curtains in a window.

GO WITH COLOR. If silver grommets aren't your style, buy colored ones or spray-paint a collection of grommets in colors that coordinate with your room.

EXPAND. Apply the process, *above*, to long curtains with large grommets attached to the top for sliding onto curtain rods. To decorate the panels, use larger grommets from boat supply stores.

what you need:

ready-made curtains

silver grommets

scissors

hammer

punching tool

THE MATCH GAME. Make misfit furniture fit in with your family of furnishings by using fabric covers. The instructions, *below,* are not specific to the chair shown *opposite;* they are general tips that you can adapt to any chair, sofa, sectional, or ottoman.

1 Measure the length and width of each component of the piece of furniture: inside back, outside back, seat, inside arm, outside arm, skirt (plus a 3-inch hem allowance).

2 Before cutting the fabric, add two inches to the length and the width measurements of each piece for seam allowances. After considering pattern repeats or a nap in the fabric, cut the back, seat, and arm pieces from the fabric with the grain. Mark the centers of each piece with a pencil or fabric-marking pen.

3 To pin the slipcover together, place right sides of the fabric against the furniture piece. Start with the top edges of the two back pieces, pinning them together using 1-inch seam allowances (see detail, *below*). Center and smooth the slipcover back on the chair; position the seat piece, matching its center to the center of the seat back. Continue the process, adding the arms and shaping the fabric sections to the contours of the piece of furniture; clip seam allowances as needed for a smooth fit.

4 When the slipcover is pinned together, carefully remove it

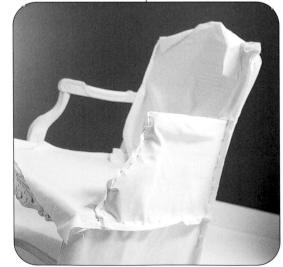

from the furniture piece and stitch the seams, using the pins as your stitching guide.

5 For a final fit and the addition of a skirt (optional), put the slipcover on the furniture piece right side out. Check corners for further clipping at seam allowances (don't snip through the stitching line). Remove from furniture piece. Measure the finished length and width of each skirt section. Hem them to the correct length, leaving 1-inch seam allowances for stitching to the body of the slipcover. Pin the skirt to the slipcover; stitch, right sides together. Trim seams to $\frac{1}{2}$ inch. Press.

what you need:

fabric
(8–10 yards of 48-inch-wide fabric for a sofa;
3–4 yards for a chair)

measuring tape

silk pins

scissors

sewing machine

thread

DIVIDE A ROOM to increase its function—and do it with style. The nooks and crannies of these bookcases are packed with objects. Add-on casters offer flexibility. Because the units roll, they can respond quickly when duty calls them elsewhere.

1 Choose furniture units to fit your spaces. Bookcases are best when they top out a couple of feet below the ceiling. This prevents tipping and keeps the space from feeling cut off from the light. Keep purpose in mind when you are shopping. For example, to separate a living and dining space, select shelves or cabinets to house pretty collectibles, as well as linens and videos. Look for flat-bottomed bookcase units to accommodate casters.

2 Follow the recommendations on the caster packages to buy the proper size for the furniture pieces. Using a drill, fasten the casters to the bottoms of the bookcases.

3 For a finished look that coordinates with your decorating scheme, cover the backs of the cases with fabric. Fold the fabric edges under, pull the panels taut, and attach with upholstery tacks.

what you need:

furniture units with flat bottoms

fabric to cover the backs of units

casters

drill/screwdriver

upholstery tacks

hammer

BLACK-AND-WHITE PHOTOCOPIES fastened to the back of a bookcase provide impactful backdrops for a favorite object or two. On some shelves, they star as works of art. To organize many items in niches, leave some spaces undecorated.

1 Find bold black-and-white flower photos or graphic photos featuring a basic nature form with a contrasting solid-color background. Seashells, stones, and simple flower faces work well. You can find them on greeting cards in art supply stores. Or use your camera to photograph your own images.

2 Have a photocopy store or a business that specializes in graphics enlarge your images to a size slightly larger than the size of the backs of your display cases.

3 Ask the copy center to glue the images to ¼-inch-thick foam core or glue the images to foam core yourself, *below.*

4 Use tacks to attach the images to the backs of open shelves. If your shelves have backs, use a paper cutter or utility knife (or ask the photocopy store for cutting help) to trim the copies slightly larger than the openings. Press the copies against the backs of the openings—they should fit snugly without glue.

what you need:

two-color images

¼-inch-thick foam core

spray adhesive

large paper cutter
or utility knife

tacks (optional)

EASY PIECES. With three boards, you can make this simple side table from birch veneer plywood. Hinge two of the pieces together to form table legs; place the third piece on top. For convenience, it folds up to a mere three inches thick and packs away.

1 Cut the wood into three equal parts with each piece measuring 22 × 11½ inches.

2 Sand the edges and surfaces smooth.

3 Finish the edges and surfaces with stain or tung oil.

4 For the table "legs," join two of the wood pieces at the long edges with the piano hinge.

5 Open the hinged section to a wide V and stand it up vertically. Place the third piece on top of it.

OPTION. As it is, the table is flexible and easy to fold up and move around. However, if objects on top are not arranged in a balanced way, the top can flip off. To stabilize the table-top, drill holes through the top and into the hinged section. Screw the top and bottom together.

what you need:

22-inch-wide × 34½-inch-long × 1-inch-thick birch veneer plywood board

14½-inch-long piano hinge

saw

drill/screwdriver

sandpaper

stain or tung oil

screws (optional)

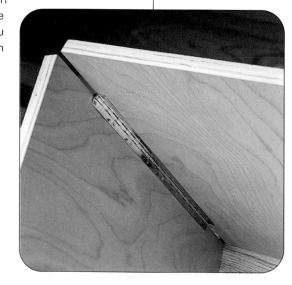

LOW-TACK, HIGH-TOUCH. Don't let a plain bedside table disappear into the woodwork. Give it a fanciful coat of many colors while still maintaining its woody undertones.

1 With low-tack painter's tape (and a ruler to make sure your tape lines are straight), mask off a border around the edge of the tabletop. Make the border as wide or narrow as desired. Use a utility knife to trim the corners where the tape intersects for clean paint edges when the tape is removed. Paint outside the tape edge and under the table edge with acrylic paint. Add a second or third coat as needed. Remove tape.

2 Inside the newly painted (and dried) border, mask off variously sized and placed squares with tape and ruler. You don't need to trim the tape edges because you paint inside the squares (see photograph, *below*). Paint inside the squares. Add second or third coats as needed.

3 Spray-paint the drawer knob with silver paint, following the manufacturer's directions. Paint the drawer front with a coordinating color.

4 Tape off the edges of the table legs and paint them.

5 When dry, cover the tabletop with one or two light coats of varnish to protect the design.

what you need:

plain wood table with drawer

low-tack painter's tape

ruler

utility knife

acrylic paints

silver spray paint

paintbrush

gloss varnish

HEAD OF THE CLASS. This veneer plywood headboard has beautiful whirls and burly swirls highlighted by two coats of shiny, see-through polyurethane. The only thing difficult about this project might be getting the board home—but what are friends for?

1 Have the home center cut your sheet of birch veneer plywood so the length is 6 inches wider than your bed. (The plywood will be attached lengthwise to your bed frame, and the 4-foot width is the headboard height.)

2 Sand the board smooth with medium-grit sandpaper. Wipe it clean with a tack cloth.

3 Apply two coats of polyurethane in a well-ventilated area, letting the first coat dry before applying the second.

4 To secure the headboard to the bed, drill holes in the lower corners of the plywood to line up with the holes in your bed frame. Attach the headboard to the frame with nuts and bolts threaded through the holes.

what you need:

4 × 8-foot sheet of ¾-inch birch plywood

medium-grit sandpaper

tack cloth

clear polyurethane

brush

nuts and bolts

drill

THE BIG BAND. One horizontal band of paint on the wall powers up the vibe for a cool, contemporary space and sets the tone for adding accents. After the stripe hits the wall, you'll feel the urge to repeat the color elsewhere in the room to balance its vitality.

1 Establish the position of the horizontal stripe on the wall, marking its top and bottom edges with short pencil marks. The stripe shown, *opposite,* is 12 inches wide; adjust the width of your stripe as you wish.

2 Place the level at the top edge of the stripe and level it. Use the edge of the level as a straightedge to continue the pencil mark outward. Repeat until the length of the top edge is marked on the wall; repeat to mark the bottom edge of the stripe.

3 Lay painter's tape along the outer edges of the stripe. Smooth the edge of the tape along the pencil line with your finger to be sure it adheres well and to prevent paint from bleeding underneath it. Leave the opposite edge of the tape loosely fastened for easy removal.

4 Paint the stripe with a paintbrush; give the stripe a second coat 4 hours later if needed. Remove the tape while the paint is wet. If the tape pulls up some of the paint along the edge, touch it up with an artist's brush.

what you need:

1 quart of latex interior wall paint in an accent color of your choice

woodworker's level

pencil

low-tack painter's tape

paintbrush

artist's brush